D0930306

PASSION WITH PURPOSE

PASSION

—— With ——

PURPOSE

The Fire Within

Building a Life of
Fulfillment, Destiny, & Impact

Steven F. Mezzacappa

NEW DEGREE PRESS

PASSION WITH PURPOSE

The Fire Within

Building a Life of Fulfillment, Destiny, & Impact

ISBN

978-1-63676-438-2   *Hardcover*

To the Great Architect, The Great Physician, and the Great Life Coach – The Alpha and the Omega – The Great I Am. To Him who was and is and ever will be – To Him who ignites, fuels, and sustains my passion – Jesus Christ – Emmanuel

CONTENTS

———

PART ONE
FULFILLMENT

PART TWO
DESTINY

PART THREE

IMPACT

END MATTER

Veni Sancte Spiritus

FOREWORD

———

Have you ever asked yourself these questions?: Who am I? Why am I here? What is my purpose in life? If so, then Steven Mezzacappa's book, Passion With Purpose: The Fire Within, is for you!

Endued with an anointing of wisdom from on High, Steven will awaken you to principles of applied Truth that are deeply personal to your experiences in life, and with each turn of the page, he will navigate you through it.

Geographic navigation on Earth is usually plotted by selecting the shortest distance between two points, with the primary goal of getting from point A to point B as quickly as possible regardless of what happens on the way.

Passion With Purpose is an exciting adventure that will awaken places within you that you never knew existed. Your spirit will be inspired, your soul will be roused, and your potential for achievement will be expanded beyond what you previously thought possible!

The Passion With Purpose journey is much more than what is experienced around you. It is the amazing revelation the Holy Spirit brings forth from within you. It is not just about your journey through life. Passion With Purpose is about the journey through your heart.

Good books are often described as "page turners" because the reader can't wait for what's coming next. This book is a page burner, as it stokes the fire of motivation within you to help you take the necessary action to overcome the spirit of fear that haunts all humanity.

The author's personal story of pain combined with his passionate presentation will enlighten you to places within your heart you previously tried to forget. Steven will show you that painful experiences are not intended to get in your way; rather, they are designed to show you the perfect plan God has for you in the days ahead.

You will see that even the most deeply painful experiences are not to be hidden and not to be concealed, nor denied or artificially medicated. Painful events are the spiritual pathway to Godly wisdom if you are willing to courageously walk through them. It is on the other side that you shall see "things too wonderful that you knew not" (Job 42:3). Passion With Purpose is the catalytic experience you have been waiting for.

Many how-to books give the reader specific sequential instructions regarding how the author accomplished certain lofty goals that exceeded his previous expectations. The problem is that every reader is uniquely different, and one author's perspective cannot be transmitted to others on a large scale without taking into consideration the individual differences of each reader.

Passion With Purpose is not another how-to instruction manual. It allows you to rightly apply the Truth right where you are in life's journey. From there, you will be challenged chapter after chapter to learn how God sees you, how God leads you, and most importantly, how God transforms you from the inside out.

Steven is careful to sift out man-centered opinions from God-inspired Truth. Opinions are finite while Truth is infinite, with the power to transform the spirit, soul, and body.

Therefore, when Truth goes forth, it is capable of universal application into the hearts of all readers.

It is often said that one cannot lead you to a place he himself has never gone. You're in good hands with Steven as your guide and Passion With Purpose as your roadmap. Enjoy the ride!

Dominic P. Herbst, MA, MS
Founder and President of Restoring Relationships
Nationally Renowned Author, Speaker,
Consultant, and Christian Psychologist

PREFACE

Dear Friend,

It brings great joy to my soul that you are holding this book in your hands. Nestled within these pages are words I hope will give inspiration, encouragement, and empowerment to some of the deepest places of your being and help you understand and grow in your relationship with God.

Perhaps the greatest challenge in writing this book was first discerning who the specific audience would be. However, as I have come to learn through the process of writing this book, it is not specifically geared toward a specific age, career field, or stage of life.

This book is designed to meet you where you presently are in your life and spiritual journey. Though the title of this book includes Building a Life of Fulfillment, Destiny, & Impact, I must be honest and say that this book is not intended to make one feel good or hear what one so desires to hear.

In fact, the most important goal of writing this book was to keep it rooted and grounded in biblical scripture, principle, and teachings. Truth is hard to come by these days, and Amazon is already overrun with self-help books that market ways to have a better and more fulfilling life.

It may surprise readers to know the teaching and writings within this book are principles I have yet to master myself and at times are hard to accept as truth and reality. This is because many of the principles in this book may be quite contrary to the teachings and guidance of modern Western culture and society.

Building a life of fulfillment, destiny, and impact has not so much to do with what we have or how much we accomplish in life; rather, a fulfilling, significant, and impactful life is truly dependent upon the depth and health of our relationship with God and others.

As you read through this book, I encourage you to reflect, journal, and discuss its principles within your community. I have provided reflection and discussion questions for each chapter toward the back of the book.

Most importantly, while you read be sure to seek out the Lord's voice and the ways He may be inviting you to go deeper with Him as He becomes the shepherd of your passion.

Wherever this book finds you, may the grace and peace of our loving Creator be with you as you embark on a journey to build a life of fulfillment, destiny, and impact, by inviting

Him into your heart to be the igniter, cultivator, and sustainer of your passion—the fire within.

I'm excited for you to be on this journey with me.

With Love & Passion,
Steven F. Mezzacappa

INTRODUCTION

Overwhelmed and troubled, He walked deeper into the Garden. As He fell on His face to pray, these words came forth from the depths of His soul: "I am so overwhelmed with sorrow, even to the point of death."

Even with several of His disciples only a stone's throw away, He was burdened with loneliness, rejection, and anxiety.

The hour has come for Jesus to fulfill His destiny.

Imagine for a moment if God allowed you to have a glimpse of your future and everything required to uncover your purpose and make the difference in the world He has called on you to complete.

Imagine if, in order to fulfill your destiny, you were required to withstand seasons of loneliness, emotional sorrow to the point of death, physical pain and suffering, despair, depression, anxiety, rejection, persecution, betrayal, being misunderstood, isolated, abandoned, and forsaken.

Would you proceed?

Would you willingly walk through each of these experiences to make a difference leading to a life of fulfillment, destiny, and impact, which culture promises us we will obtain, if we follow our passions and purpose to make a difference in the world?

Before Jesus endured His crucifixion, He spent His final night preparing to fulfill His destiny. Being fully man and fully divine, He knew every detail that would ensue. He knew the level and depths of pain He was about to endure—not only physically, but emotionally as well. He also knew the reward and impact of His destiny, yet was still overrun with sadness, anxiety, loneliness, and rejection. Despite knowing His suffering would lead to salvation for humanity, He still pleaded with God, "My Father, if all things are possible, let this cup pass from me."

The moments after Jesus prayed in the Garden of Gethsemane up until His crucifixion have been accounted as "the Passion" by theologians and Christians for centuries. If we look at the word "passion" through a modern cultural lens, we would find this term interestingly misleading.

Modern Western culture today promises us that if we simply follow our passions and the desires of our heart, we will experience a life of fulfillment, destiny, and impact. I'm writing this book because it's time to actually talk about what passion truly is and how it impacts you and those around you.

Passion is not simply something that can be chased; in actuality, passion is something you experience. Deeper than the action itself, passion is the thought, feeling, and choice experienced while doing the action.

This revelation is important to ponder because if we were to live our life by simply following our culture's definition of "passion," we would be led to quit the moment we encountered pain, suffering, or sorrow on our journey. Our culture makes passion about us, whereas God makes passion about the betterment of others.

It's important to distinguish our culture's view of passion from a biblical view of passion. To define the difference now and throughout the rest of this book, I will borrow a couple words from theologian Watchman Nee: *soulical* and *soulish*.[1] These words will be defined more deeply, but for now, a *soulical passion* is a passion that is rooted in love and truth and ignited, sustained, and equipped by God's spirit while a *soulish passion* is a passion that is rooted in fear and pain and attempts to be sustained by one's own soul.

A *soulical passion* is God's passion, whereas a *soulish passion* is "self" passion.

* * *

Purpose is often associated with making a difference externally in another person, but culture takes the feeling of fulfillment experienced when impacting another and idolizes this feeling of ecstasy. We are then led to live for the feeling rather than the impact.

Imagine if Jesus lived for the feeling rather than the impact and result of His calling. If Jesus lived for the feeling, maybe

---

1   Watchman Nee, *The Spiritual Man* (New York: Christian Fellowship Publishers, Inc, 1977), 6.

He may not have continued on the path forward—the path that led to salvation for mankind.

You see, passion is fleeting and misleading and the human heart is deceitful and difficult to truly understand (Jeremiah 17:9).

Building a life of fulfillment, destiny, and impact isn't about you and me. Rather, it is about God and the people around you. We should be hesitant to follow our passion and instead follow our Spirit without the influence of our thoughts, feelings, and choices.

I've experienced the wrath and result of following a passion for life that was driven by emotion as opposed to being guided by intuition.

Growing up, I was on a mission to change the world by inspiring others using the lessons I learned through my personal accomplishments. I wanted others to know anything was possible based on what I could overcome and achieve.

I had a passion for buildings and my biggest dream in life was to build skyscrapers around the world. I spent my entire high school and college career chasing this passion, only to find out during my last summer before graduating college this passion would be met with an overwhelming sense of sadness, sorrow, and disappointment.

I spent the first twenty-two years of my life following my passion and making a difference to only end up burdened with thoughts of despair, losing all hope in myself and in any dreams I once had.

But one desperate day during my fall semester I scribbled these words in my journal while sitting in class: "God I beg you. . .Please come to me. Fill my heart. . .Be kindle in me. . . the fire of your love. Lord I beg you. Heal my heart. My heart is yours. Help. . ."

By God's grace and goodness, He answered the call and from that moment and the moments that followed, my life would forever change, continuing to be molded and shaped by God even now.

Wherever you find yourself in your walk with God, it's my deep desire that you read this book with an open mind. Whether you are newer to the faith or have been a practicing Christian for some time, I invite you to read this book and critique it through a biblical lens.

Let not my words teach you, but let my words help you invite the Holy Spirit's teaching and leading, for the Bible is and always will be sufficient (2 Timothy 3:16). It's simply my hope this book can serve as a guide in helping you, dear friend, uncover the divine blueprints to build a life of fulfillment, destiny, and impact through a deeper relationship with God.

It breaks my heart when I see others preaching that life is meant to be full of happiness without any suffering involved. If this was the case, what does that mean for the people who do suffer daily in areas where they physically do not have control? Are their lives of any less value than yours?

Like Jesus, we are called to experience suffering. We are called to experience passion. We are called to walk forward despite what our thoughts, feelings, and choices tell us. Not simply for our own good, but for the good of others around us.

The question that remains is, how do we persevere in spite of adversity and pain? How do we take the cup we so desire to pass from us?

The answer lies in that of human passion—something we value so much, yet truly know very little about.

To help us uncover the relationship between passion and purpose and how this intersection can serve as a blueprint to building a life of fulfillment, destiny, and impact, this book is intentionally broken down into three parts.

PART 1 – FULFILLMENT – BUILDING A LIFE INSPIRED BY THE GREAT ARCHITECT

Part 1 inspires us to look at an alternative definition of passion. It defines passion as not something we follow, but something we experience, build, and cultivate within ourselves. When it comes to having a fulfilling life, it's not so much about what we have, but who we have and understanding what builds up or tears down the passion within our hearts, in spite of any season we find ourselves in.

PART 2 – DESTINY – BUILDING A LIFE ENCOURAGED BY THE GREAT PHYSICIAN

Part 2 encourages us to learn how our passion can be driven by fear or led by love. Throughout our lives, we will be dealt emotional wounds, which, if left unhealed, can serve as the engine for the actions and dreams we set up for our lives. By being led into love by the Great Physician, it is a passion that is reconciled, restored, and fostered by Jesus that leads us to our destiny.

PART 3 – IMPACT – BUILDING A LIFE EMPOWERED BY THE GREAT LIFE COACH

Part 3 empowers us to make a difference in the lives of others around us by learning how to be led and guided by the Great Life Coach, the Holy Spirit. We are equipped with the tools to not only build up the fire within ourselves, but also build up the fire and passion within those around us so that in spite of any adversity or challenge, we and others can live out the callings and purpose in our lives with a passion that never burns out.

* * *

As we proceed forth in life doing the best we can to build a fulfilling, significant, and impactful life, we may find ourselves asking the same question Jesus asked God in the Garden of Gethsemane, "My Father, if it is possible, may this cup be taken from me?"

When we find ourselves in this position, with our calling uncovered, will we respond like Jesus did and despite the adversities of life, also respond to God, "Yet not my will, but yours be done?"

Dear friends, a life of fulfillment, destiny, and impact isn't measured by how much we accomplish of our own will in this fallen world; instead, it is measured by love and how we walk into the fullness of who God created us to be and what He has called us to.

A life of fulfillment, destiny, and impact is the intersection of love, authenticity, and obedience.

Let your passion be the engine to accomplish God's plans for your life, not a distraction. The message within this book is one that helped me loosen the shackles of depression and uncover a renewed vision and hope for life—a hope far greater than any material possession or accomplishment can offer in this world.

It's my prayer that the message of hope and truth in this book inspires, encourages, and empowers you to build a life of fulfillment, destiny, and impact by building a life inspired by the Great Architect, encouraged by the Great Physician, and empowered by the Great Life Coach.

PART ONE

FULFILLMENT

*BUILDING A LIFE INSPIRED BY
THE GREAT ARCHITECT*

Let us look up to God the Father as the Great
Architect of Creation and be awakened to
His blueprints to build a life of fulfillment.

CHAPTER 1

DON'T FOLLOW YOUR PASSION

———

So flee youthful passions and pursue righteousness,
faith, love, and peace, along with those who
call on the Lord from a pure heart.

- 2 TIMOTHY 2:22 (ESV)

It was a cold, drizzly day in "Happy Valley" at Penn State's Beaver Stadium on Homecoming Weekend. I had the great honor of being one of the students on PSU Homecoming 2016's Student Court, an honor bestowed to just ten graduating seniors. As the tradition goes, at halftime, the Student Court gets the honor of being recognized on the field in front of a crowd of one hundred thousand-plus students and spectators.

I just wanted to see the excitement that filled the stadium. I just wanted to feel the joy of this moment. I just wanted to walk with conviction and pride in my accomplishments. I just wanted to be present and happy, but I couldn't.

Everything within me and around me was numb. I was looking, but I could not see. I was smiling, but I could not feel. I was walking, but I could not direct my steps. I was numb. The only thought I could process was that I would one day speak about this experience to help give hope to the brokenhearted.

I was in the fifth and final year of my architectural engineering program, and few know that in the hours leading up to this moment in Beaver Stadium, I snuck away from the tailgates and hid in the Porta Potties to try and process the pain I was going through. I begged God for mercy while I cried and pleaded for peace. At this point, the light of hope in my life was dimming, and the passion I had for life was completely burnt out.

By the time my last year of college rolled around, I had achieved everything I could have dreamed of and more from society's viewpoint of success. I had served as the president for three different organizations on campus, been a captain twice for the world's largest student-run philanthropy, and was tapped into two of PSU's senior honor societies. I was even nationally recognized in the nation as the New Face of Civil Engineering the previous spring.

To top it off, I had a job offer in hand to start my career with one of the country's largest construction management firms and was given the choice to choose where I would start my career, including the option to start it internationally—a dream I have had since I was just a child.

I was accomplished and was achieving every dream I had set for myself and more. I was also back for my final year, coming off a summer where I had just lived out a childhood dream of working on an international skyscraper project in Mexico City.

How can I have accomplished all of this, yet be depressed?

On paper, I had the perfect college experience and the perfect life. But deep down within me was a soul breathing its last breath. I had been known by others for my passion for life, but what others didn't know, myself included, was that the passion I was living was not a healthy passion. It was a passion that was contagious and impacted many positively, but it was self destructive, filled with holes and voids buried deep. It lit up the souls of others but burned mine. It was all consuming and unsustainable.

Not even the shouts of one hundred thousand people in Penn State's Beaver Stadium could breathe life back into my soul.

It felt as though I experienced a "soul death" during my final year of college as I battled suicidal ideation on a daily basis.

Despite the darkness around me and within me, I had no one to turn to but God.

LOOKING UP

I had spent my entire academic life leading up to college in Catholic school and knew a lot about God, theology, and religion. I just didn't know who God was. I didn't know Jesus personally.

I lived my life having a surface-level relationship with Jesus. I believed "I could do all things through Christ who strengthens me," as Philippians 4:13 coins. I thought by being successful and by making a difference I was doing God's work. I thought having a relationship with God required my works themselves and not simply me.

And that is how I lived the first twenty-two years of my life. I was going to change the world doing what I loved. I was going to serve. I was going to make others laugh and smile. I was going to inspire others. I was going to help others find their passion. I was going to help others find their purpose.

I . . . I . . . I . . .

It was all about me and my vision for life; the question I posed before God was, "How can You help me live out my vision?"

I was living as though God was a part of my story, not as though I was a part of His.

I can now see how pride echoed throughout my soul, but I never saw it back then. In our culture, it's common to link pride with arrogance and hubris, but I always sought to speak with humility, not realizing pride isn't simply about how we are viewed in light of others—it can also be how we view ourselves in light of God.

Is God helping us do what we want to do in life? Or are we helping God do what He wants to do in our life? Is God intersecting our story? Are we intersecting His story? Is passion and purpose about us? Or is passion and purpose about God and others?

REDEFINING PASSION

We have been taught by our culture to follow our passion above all else in this world, as if this "passion" is a noun, something discovered outside of ourselves. However, if you look up the etymology of the word passion to uncover its history, how it originated, and what it literally means, would you still want to "follow your passion?"

In Latin, passion comes from the words pati and passionem, meaning to endure, undergo, experience, and suffer, respectively.[2] There is an intentional reason why the crucifixion of Jesus Christ is referred to as His passion. It refers to the suffering Jesus experienced not only physically, but internally as well.

In his book The Passion and the Cross, Father Ron Rolheiser goes a little deeper into the word passion as it relates to Jesus's suffering on the cross. Building on the etymology of the word, Father Rolheiser notes that "passion comes from the Latin passio meaning passiveness, non-activity, absorbing something more than actively doing anything."[3]

Passion spans beyond the physical realm and deeper into the internal realm. We experience passion in our thought life, our emotional life, and in our volitional life.

As Jesus suffered the physical agonies of the crucifixion, He also experienced the burdens of loneliness, rejection, and

---

2   Online Etymology Dictionary, s.v. "passion (n.)," accessed January 13, 2021.

3   Ronald Rolheiser, *The Passion and the Cross* (Cincinnati: Franciscan Media, 2015), 1.

anxiety. The fruit of these pains root themselves internally, and for many, we may say this pain is in our heart and mind, but when we define our internal being as only our heart or mind, we leave out the beauty and complexity of our inner and deepest self.

Traditionally, many people contextualize the human person from a dualistic perspective and as a dichotomy comprised of body and mind, with the body being our physical being and the mind being our internal being.[4]

Others view the human person from a tripartite perspective, and as having a trichotomy, composed of not only a body and mind, but also a spirit as well.[5]

As a trichotomy, it is understood that the human person is both a physical and spiritual being. Even in dichotomy, some view the mind as the spiritual part of a person; however, this view is limited in understanding the depths and intricacy of the inner and spiritual self.

1 Thessalonians 5:23 uses three distinct words to describe the whole person: spirit, soul, and body. Even in its original Greek text, three distinctive words were used: pneuma (spirit), psuche (soul), and soma (body).[6] This biblical perception of the person as tripartite is profound because where the traditional understanding of trichotomy uses mind, the Bible uses soul.

---

4   Nee, *The Spiritual Man*, 21.

5   Ibid.

6   Bible Hub, s.v. "1 Thessalonians 5:23," accessed January 13, 2021.

Figure 1.1: An Illustration of 1 Thessalonians
5:23 by Steven F. Mezzacappa

Interestingly enough, the word psychology comes from the word psyche, which comes from psuche.[7] How interesting is it that despite the fact that psychology means the study of the soul, it is more commonly understood as "study of the mind?"[8] The mind is in fact, just one faculty of the human soul.[9]

Along with many other theologians, Watchman Nee, in his book The Spiritual Man, teaches the human soul embodies three main faculties: intellect (or mind), emotion, and will

---

7   Bible Hub, s.v. "5590. psuche," accessed January 13, 2021.

8   Online Etymology Dictionary, s.v. "Psychology (n.)," accessed January 13, 2021.

9   Nee, The Spiritual Man, 30.

(or volition).[10] For consistency throughout this book, we will reference the three faculties of the soul as intellect, emotion, and will. We will dive deeper into each of these elements throughout the course of the book and use the following definitions for them:

🔥 Our Intellect is our organ of thought

🔥 Our Emotion is our organ of feeling

🔥 Our Will is our organ of choice

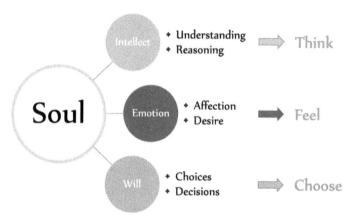

Figure 1.2: Functions of the Soul by Steven F. Mezzacappa
with inspiration from Watchman Nee[11]

With our thoughts, feelings, and choices in mind, it is important to note that this is where we internally process both the outside physical world and spiritual realm. Within

10   Ibid., 35–38.

11   Ibid., 35–38.

our soul lies the revelation of understanding, the stimulation of our deepest affections or afflictions, and the consequence of decision.

Within our soul we think. Within our soul we feel. Within our soul we choose.

It is within our soul that we experience passion. Our passion is not something found or discovered outside of who we are. Our passion is who we are.

Intricate, malleable, and alive, our passion has the ability to drive us or lead us.

Reactive and responsive, our passion isn't solely experienced; it is also fostered.

Like electricity generating light, so too does one's spirit animate the soul.[12] Our soul is a product of what we feed it. Like a fire is the product of oxygen, heat, and fuel, so too is our soul the product of intellect, emotion, and will.

Our passion is the fire within us.

THE FIRE WITHIN US

With passion being the fire within us, it is that energy within us reacting to our experiences and relationships. It's intentional, living, breathing, and alive, requiring cultivation and care within communion and community.

---

12   Ibid., 25.

Our thoughts, feelings, and choices are shaped by our experiences and relationships with others. It's important to take note of this because when thoughts are coupled with feelings, they become attitudes and thus influence our behaviors, as modern psychologists note in the Cognitive Behavioral Model.[13] Our passion, therefore, can be something that propels us forward, energizing us, or holds us in bondage, draining us.

In life, we may not have control over what happens to us, but we do have control over how we process, within our souls, the events and circumstances we experience. I mention this all to preface and qualify the discussion of what happens to us when we experience some level of emotional trauma in our lives.

Just as physical trauma and wounds need time and therapy to heal, so too do our emotional traumas. If not dealt with properly and if not properly given the right treatment, we can find ourselves self-medicating.

Self-medication is often associated with alcohol abuse or illicit substance use, often leaving out the plethora of other ways to self-medicate. In fact, following our passion can be a form of self-medication. Many say time heals all wounds, but that is only relevant if the proper treatment is administered in conjunction with time.

Let's say you cut your arm, for example. If you don't apply any ointment, you risk that cut getting worse with time, perhaps

---

13 "The Cognitive Behavioral Model," *Therapist Aid*, accessed January 13, 2021.

even infected. The same goes for an emotional cut on one's soul. As time progresses without any "ointment" or therapy, we risk the case of an infected soul.

Later in part two of this book, we will have a whole chapter dedicated to the infected soul and how detrimental that can be to one's passion. I make mention of it early here in Chapter One as we redefine passion because this will serve as another foundational principle for this book.

SOULICAL VS. SOULISH PASSION

In the introductory chapter, we distinguished a healthy passion from an unhealthy passion by utilizing the terms soulical and soulish.

To dive a little deeper into these terms from the introduction, please see the two definitions below:

Soulical: "pertains to those proper, appropriate, legitimate, or natural qualities, functions, or expressions of man's soul which the Creator intended from the very beginning for the soul uniquely to possess and manifest."[14]

Soulish: describes one "who is so governed by the soulical part of his being that his whole life takes on the character and expression of the soul."[15]

---

14   Watchman Nee, *The Spiritual Man* (New York: Christian Fellowship Publishers, Inc, 1977), 6.

15   Ibid.

These terms will be used throughout the remainder of the book, and we will discuss them in much greater detail, but for now, the main key to keep in mind is that we should desire to build a life with a soulical passion.

A soulical passion is a passion that is ignited, fueled, and sustained by God. With this form of passion, the expressions of intellect, emotion, and will are divinely sustained and guided by God's Spirit. It is a passion that roots itself in truth and God's perfect will for our lives.

A soulish passion is a passion that is dominated and misguided fully by one's intellect, emotion, and will in their fallen nature. This type of passion is truly driven by one's emotions rather than being guided by God's Spirit, and it is truly fueled by selfish motives.

Soulish passion is something we follow that quenches the Spirit, while soulical passion is something we build and through which we experience the fullness of the Spirit pouring into our soul to guide it, sustain it, and give it strength.

WHY I FOLLOWED PASSION

I lived a fortunate childhood, but like many I had walked through some adverse circumstances. Between undergoing a couple seasons of bullying, living through my parent's divorce at a young age, and experiencing the collateral pain of my father's battle with addiction, the seeds of rejection and low self-worth were planted at an early age. But when you are a young kid, especially a boy, no one tells you how to process or deal with your emotions. The only way you are taught to deal with your emotions is to get over them.

So that's what I did. From an early age I told myself this was my moment to overcome adversity and pursue success. From middle school to high school, I chased success and ambition with everything inside of me. The pain deep within me that I didn't know was there went with me to college, where I experienced even more success. All of my accomplishments brought about personal glory, attention, and opportunity—great remedies for a soul that had been deeply wounded.

There's more to unpack, but I bring all this up to illustrate how the experiences you walk through in life shape how you interact with the world and make imprints on your soul. Whether it is a positive or negative experience, it becomes a part of who you are and how you perceive the outside world and develop your personal worldview, in addition to how you think, feel, and choose as you proceed forth with action.

THE COST OF FOLLOWING PASSION

Despite living in a culture where we are told from a young age following our passion will result in a fulfilling life, statistics show a growing sense of unhappiness at work and a rise in struggles with mental health.

Only less than 50 percent of US workers feel they are in good jobs.[16]

---

16   Jack Kelly, "More Than Half of US Workers Are Unhappy in Their Jobs: Here's Why and What Needs to Be Done Now," *Forbes*, October 25, 2019.

Depression ranks among the top three workplace problems for employee assistance professionals, following only family crisis and stress.[17]

Depression costs over $51 billion in absenteeism from work and lost productivity and $26 billion in direct treatment costs.[18]

Nearly one in five Americans over the age of eighteen is affected by anxiety disorders.[19]

About 10 percent of youth in the US have severe depression.[20]

Depression is the most common health problem for college students.[21]

Around 31 percent of college students have seriously considered suicide.[22]

From 1999 through 2018, the suicide rate increased 35 percent.[23]

---

17 "Depression in The Workplace," Mental Health America, accessed January 13, 2021.

18 Ibid.

19 "Facts & Statistics," Anxiety and Depression Association of America, accessed January 13, 2021.

20 "Mental Health In America - Printed Reports," Mental Health America, accessed January 13, 2021.

21 "Depression & College Students," Affordable Colleges Online, accessed January 13, 2021.

22 Ibid.

23 "Increase in Suicide Mortality in the United States, 1999–2018," Centers for Disease Control and Prevention, accessed January 13, 2021.

One's identity correlates significantly with mental health. When we tell, guide, and mentor others to "follow their passion," it is implied our passion is something outside ourselves and this thing outside ourselves is our identity and doesn't change.

The issue with this is that as the seasons change, so too does the world around us and our environment. If my passion and identity is my job, what happens if I get laid off? If my passion is my hobby for art, what happens when I wake up one day and it just isn't fun anymore?

Experiencing a life of fulfillment, destiny, and impact isn't something found by following stimulated emotions; rather, it is something we create by building passion. In the same way that the tallest buildings around the world require strong, resilient, and permanent foundations, our life requires a passion built on a supernatural foundation cemented in divine truth, bonded together by divine love, and guided firmly by divine guidance.

Passion is the fuel and energy for every
person that communicates.

- JOHN C. MAXWELL[24]

---

24 John Maxwell and Mark Cole, "Transformational Leadership (Part 1)," February 3, 2021, in *The John Maxwell Leadership Podcast*, produced by John C. Maxwell, podcast, MP3 audio, 34:58.

CHAPTER 2

BUILD YOUR PASSION

———

Therefore everyone who hears these words of mine and puts them into practice is like a wise man who built his house on the rock. The rain came down, the streams rose, and the winds blew and beat against that house; yet it did not fall, because it had its foundation on the rock. But everyone who hears these words of mine and does not put them into practice is like a foolish man who built his house on sand. The rain came down, the streams rose, and the winds blew and beat against that house, and it fell with a great crash.

- MATTHEW 7:24-27

From an early age I loved construction. There was something about wearing work boots, getting dirty, and working with tools. It was like food for my soul. Before my parents' divorce, my dad built homes and my mom often brought me to visit him and his projects. Even before I could swing a hammer, I resorted to happily throwing out garbage, sweeping the floors of the house with a broom, and, if there was nothing else I was old enough to do, I would sneak away, grab a shovel, and dig random holes in the front yard or backyard.

My "passion" for building was within me for as long as I could remember. Like many young boys growing up, I wanted to be just like my dad.

But shortly after the separation of my parents, my passion for building began to increase. At that time and for most of my adolescent years, I didn't know why, but it was almost as if my passion took a hold of me. As early as ten, I began to build these intricate and detailed houses out of popsicle sticks, and then I would cover the house with cardboard as you would use plywood to enclose a home.

I'd then decorate these homes similar to the homes that meant a lot to me. One home in particular took some inspiration from one of the homes where my dad lived, and another was based on my aunt's home a few blocks away. Detailed and intricate, these little miniature "perfect" homes garnered praise and adoration from many friends and family members around me.

I heard things like, "You should be an architect," "You're going to be an engineer," and "You'd be a great builder one day."

Hearing these words of affirmation served as a remedy for the broken heart I carried around. Back then, these words affirmed to me my calling in life, but looking back, they actually affirmed the pain that had been building within me as a result of my dad's absence in my life. Between being teased and bullied at school and internalizing my father's struggle with addiction, I felt accepted when I heard this encouragement from loved ones.

In eighth grade, I began to become obsessed with math and science—not because I was a mathematician or scientist by any means, but because I knew if I wanted to be a good architect or engineer one day, I would need to be good at math and science. It was almost as if I forced myself to like these subjects.

My passion grew from building houses to desiring to build tall skyscrapers. It was as early as eighth grade when I vowed I would design and build the world's tallest skyscraper one day. It wasn't too long after that when I started to take the Staten Island Ferry into Manhattan to be struck by the awe and wonder of its buildings. I regularly walked by the World Trade Center site to see the rebuilding take place. Often on my strolls throughout lower Manhattan, I daydreamed about one day constructing buildings like the ones I saw and encountered Turner Construction signs on many project sites. This is a company I want to work for someday, I regularly thought to myself.

This dream came true as early as my freshman year of college, when I landed a summer internship with this company. I went on to intern each summer while attending Penn State, and my last summer internship was with the company's international group in Mexico City. This had been a dream of mine from the time I was young and simply building popsicle stick houses. I so desired to travel the world building skyscrapers.

Interestingly enough, the project I worked on while in Mexico was a fifty-story skyscraper, the Torre BBVA Bancomer. I was just twenty-two at the time, and here I was wandering around the streets of Mexico City doing CrossFit, exploring the country's marvelous cities on the weekends, and living out a lifelong dream during the week. Sounds incredible, right? I sure made it seem incredible on my Instagram and Facebook.

What many didn't know that summer, however, was that the metaphorical skyscraper I was building for my life came crumbling down. This metaphorical building had looked beautiful, and I was just about to add the spire at the top signaling I had finally made it. I had accomplished my dream, and as I wrapped up this summer interning in Mexico City, I thought I would finish school and go on to work for my company's international group, working on buildings across the globe and enjoying this magnificent skyscraper I had built for myself.

But the reality was that this fulfilled dream experienced an earthquake powered by disappointment, a complete absence of fulfillment, and a one-way ticket to depression.

It wasn't long until I started spending evenings in my lonely hotel room wondering what on Earth I was going to do with my life. This was who I am. I'm a builder. I was born to build buildings. I was born to build skyscrapers. I was going to inspire others with what I could build. How am I depressed? Why am I depressed? Am I ungrateful? My head and thoughts spun in circles.

It felt like I had lost my identity. I had certainly lost my passion. And before my very eyes, it felt like my life was crumbling down. It was as if the foundation on which I had been building my skyscraper had been weak and shaky all along. It was as if the life I had been building for myself was like a house constructed on loose sand.

There's so much painful truth I learned from this experience, and I am excited to dissect it and share it with you throughout the course of this book. Not only did I learn we shouldn't follow our passion, I also learned we should be cautious about finding fulfillment in our passion and be wary about finding significance or meaning from our passion.

AN ALTERNATIVE PERSPECTIVE ON PASSION

In the early stages of writing this book, I sat down with one of the pastors from my church, Pastor Blaine Workman, to talk about the concept of passion. When he shared his perspective of passion, I found it both profound and remarkable.

Pastor Blaine noted passion as "the intersection of our story in God's story." Summarizing our discussion further, it was first and foremost about understanding the "why" of our intersection with God, thereby forming a relationship with God and giving birth to a renewed identity.

As I reflected on our conversation, I thought of Genesis 2:7: "And the Lord God formed man of the dust of the ground and breathed into his nostrils the breath of life; and man became a living soul" (KJV). The truth is, from the beginning of time, mankind has always been a part of God's story, and it's because of God that we have life.

Dissecting the verse above a little deeper, we should draw our attention to two words/phrases: "breath of life" and "living soul."

Mankind would not have become a living soul without the breath of life, that is, God's Spirit. Whether we want to realize it or not, we are a part of God's story. He isn't a part of ours. Furthermore, it is God's Spirit that gives life to our soul. Without the Spirit of God within us, is our soul fully alive? Is our passion fully inflamed?

Before the fall of Adam and Eve, mankind was Spirit led, meaning the soul and body were under the guidance, sovereignty, and leading of God's Spirit within them. Now, I must make clear that God wasn't controlling mankind, as we are not machines. We were and are made in the likeness of God and in God's image (Genesis 1:26-27). It is God's spirit that gives life to our spirit, thus animating the unique soul within you and me and giving us each the liberty to think with our intellect, feel with our emotions, and choose with our will.

The souls of all mankind desire three major things: a sense of belonging, the love of others, and impact within community. When the Spirit governed the soul, the passion within man and his needs for significance, love, and purpose were all fully met in a divine and perfect relationship with God.

But after the fall of man through Adam and Eve's sin in the Garden of Eden, the communion and relationship between God and man was severed, thus leaving the soul of man and its passion crushing the Spirit and governing the self. The issue with this is that our passion is fleeting and misleading as the inner self can be deceitful (Jeremiah 17:9). As we will learn throughout this book, we may have valid feelings, but we should be cautious in being led by our emotions because they may be driven by pain and fear rather than healing and love.

Because of the fall, we have also lost sight of our relationship with God. As human beings, we have a spirit nestled deep within us, but it isn't until we reconcile our relationship with God that our spirit can be quickened by the Spirit of God, which some theologians would call regeneration.[25]

---

25 Watchman Nee, *The Spiritual Man* (New York: Christian Fellowship Publishers, Inc, 1977), 31–34.

BUILDING PASSION WITHIN OUR SOUL

Our spirit, like the soul, has three faculties: intuition, communion, and conscience.[26] There is a noticeable similarity and knitting between the three faculties of the spirit and the three faculties of the soul: intuition with intellect; communion with emotion; conscience with will.

Figure 2.1: Spirit-Soul Relationship by Steven F. Mezzacappa

In his book The Spiritual Man, Watchman Nee distinguishes the relationships and differences between the intuition and mind by saying, "Intuition involves a direct sensing independent of any outside influence. That knowledge which comes to us without any help from the mind, emotion or volition (will) comes intuitively. We really

---

26   Ibid.

'know' through our intuition; our mind merely helps us to 'understand.'"[27] When we examine ourselves, it is important to know God communicates to our spirit and not directly to our soul, where our emotions and feelings lie.

Nee further describes communion as the faculty of the spirit that worships God, thereby building relationship and intimacy with God.[28] The communion we experience with God in our spirit trickles down to our soul and is expressed and experienced within our emotion.

Finally, conscience, Nee teaches, "is the discerning organ which distinguishes right and wrong."[29] This voice of right and wrong communicates down to our soul's faculty of will, empowering us and equipping us to make decisions.

Psalm 139:14 tells us we are fearfully and wonderfully made, and rightfully so. God intentionally made us in His image, having a spirit, a soul, and a body. Having an understanding that distinguishes between the spirit and soul, along with the relationship between the two, is vital to understanding what a relationship with God looks like and how we can build our passion supernaturally by way of the Spirit communicating, infilling, and breathing into the soul the life of our Creator, that being divine truth, divine love, and divine guidance.

Upon the foundations of divine truth, divine love, and divine guidance is the blueprint for a passion that will never crumble or burn out.

---

27 Nee, *The Spiritual Man,* 32.

28 Ibid.

29 Ibid.

Within the context of this discussion, it is important not to leave out the body and its impact in building or fueling passion.

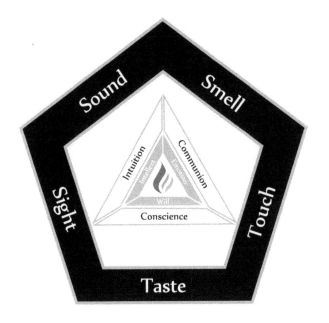

Figure 2.2: Spirit-Soul-Body Relationship

The goal of Figure 2.2 is to communicate the symmetrical and clean avenue of communication from the Spirit to the Soul. As you will see, the pentagon, which includes sound, smell, touch, taste, and sight, represents our body and is not so symmetrical with the Spirit and Soul.

We are so often looking to fill our souls and our passions with materialism and the things of this world, forgetting to realize it is not the best path to fuel or build our passion. We should be slow to build our passion with finite things that have sound, smell, touch, taste, and sight, and quick to build our passion with things that are eternal having divine truth, divine love, and divine guidance.

Another illustration that goes a little deeper on the trichotomy of man, utilizing some lessons learned from Chapter One, is the Threefold Nature of Man sketch by Rev. Clarence Larkin below.

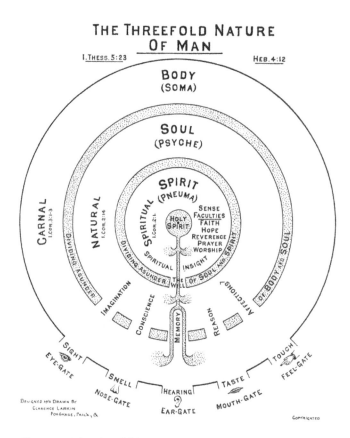

Figure 2.3: The Threefold Nature of Man by Rev. Clarence Larkin[30]

---

30   Used with permission of the Rev. Clarence Larkin Estate, P.O. Box 334, Glenside, PA 19038, U.S.A., 215-576-5590 • www.larkinestate.com

One key point to observe from Larkin's sketch is that the soul can be filled from both directions, thus making it the mediator between the spirit and the body. Through our soul's faculty of will, we have the liberty to choose what enters our soul and how it builds up our passion. Another element from Larkin's sketch illustrates how the Holy Spirit can flow into both our soul and body from the inside out, not only impacting ourselves, but those around us as well.

BUILDING PASSION WITHIN OUR BODY

Another crucial element to this discussion is the question of where the human brain lies within this context. Psychology and scientific studies of the human mind didn't truly begin until the eighteenth century.[31] Still to this day there is still so much more to unpack when it comes to the human brain and our mind.

In fact, many modern scientists hold a materialist view of the human brain. Leading communication pathologist, audiologist, and cognitive neuroscientist Dr. Caroline Leaf specializes in the difference between mind and brain and how they affect one another. In her book, Switch on Your Brain, Dr. Leaf reports the materialist view believes it is the brain that affects the mind as opposed to the mind affecting the brain. For clarification's sake here, view the mind as soul.

Materialists believe chemicals and neurons create the mind.[32] Ultimately they perceive man as a machine, crediting our

---

31   "Introduction to the Field of Psychology," Lumen Learning, accessed January 13, 2021.

32   Caroline Leaf, *Switch On Your Brain* (Grand Rapids: Baker Publishing Group, 2015), 31–32.

chemical biology with creating thoughts independent from memories and experiences in our environment. The issue with this view, however, is that we are not machines. We are spiritual beings. Our thoughts come from the mind that resides within our soul. How can chemicals dictate what you think about? I'm not claiming to be a psychiatrist here, but while brain neurology may impact how we think as it relates to rumination, when it comes to the types of thoughts we ponder, reflect on, and materialize, these come from a source deep within us and also from the outside world.

In her book, Dr. Leaf also talks about two scientific terms, epigenetics and neuroplasticity. Epigenetics refers to the "fact that your thoughts and choices impact your physical brain and body, your mental health, and your spiritual development."[33] Dr. Leaf further explains that epigenetics is the science behind how our "thoughts and emotions are transformed into physiological and spiritual effects, and then physiological experiences transform into mental and emotional states. . . something seemingly immaterial like a belief can take on a physical existence as a positive or negative change in our cells."[34]

Neuroplasticity refers to the ability of the brain to "change and regrow" based on the thoughts, emotions, and choices we entertain.[35] In other words, what we think about and the memories we develop form and take up physical space in

---

33 Ibid., 56.

34 Ibid., 14.

35 Ibid.

our brains. In addition, what we build up in our thought life, we build up within ourselves whether it be healthy or toxic.

Dr. Leaf is notorious for saying that science is finally catching up with the Bible despite the present world trying to prove itself through science alone. Dr. Leaf shared many verses from Scripture that science can now biologically and scientifically explain:

"For as he thinks in his heart, so is he." - Proverbs 23:7, NKJV

"Do not conform to the pattern of this world, but be transformed by the renewing of your mind." - Romans 12:2

"Therefore put away all filthiness and rampant wickedness and receive with meekness the implanted word, which is able to save your souls." - James 1:21, ESV

"Finally, brothers and sisters, whatever is true, whatever is noble, whatever is right, whatever is pure, whatever is lovely, whatever is admirable—if anything is excellent or praiseworthy—think about such things." - Philippians 4:8

BUILDING PASSION IS OUR RESPONSIBILITY

As demonstrated, when we expand our understanding of passion to something within us that is alive, impacted by the environment, and malleable, we are better positioned to live a life full of passion. We may not always be able to control the environments we find ourselves in, but by building passion within our being, we can rise to the occasion. Such a lesson is invaluable, because whoever said the destiny and mission of our lives was meant to be easy, simple, and free of pain was incorrect. If the Son of Man could not escape suffering, why should we think we can? If we claim to live like Christ, we must also be ready to suffer like Christ as well.

Therefore, build your passion. Build it with divine truth, divine love, and divine guidance, knowing that as you think within yourself, you are not only spiritually building up your passion, but you are also physically building it up as well.

Such a "building" as this may be hard to build alone, but as the most complex buildings ever built had architects guiding the vision, so too does the life we seek to build have a Great Architect.

At the end of the day, it is our decision. Will we build passion based on the plans developed by the ruler of this world and culture? Or will we build passion based on the plans of the Great Architect who is the Alpha and Omega, the maker of Heaven and Earth?

CHAPTER 3

THE GREAT ARCHITECT & HIS BLUEPRINTS

———

So get rid of all the filth and evil in your lives, and humbly accept the word God has planted in your hearts, for it has the power to save your souls.

- JAMES 1:21, NLT

The world we live in offers many drawings and blueprints to build a life that answers our deepest needs and desires, but deep down we know these answers are never good enough to fill the divine need nestled deep within our souls and build the life that we so desperately desire.

Since 2013, I've been fortunate enough to have worked for one of the world's largest construction companies. During my career, I've worked on projects including skyscrapers, a major hospital, a sports stadium, and a large pharmaceutical facility. Though these projects have spanned different industries and building types, one commonality was the authority of the project's contract and drawings.

Whenever there was a question or dispute among subcontractors, team members could rest assured and always consult the drawings for direction. Often though, the drawings were never mostly complete or perfect, and when this was the case, team members would be led to reach out to the developer of the drawing set, the project's architect. This process has been formally termed the RFI process for decades, with RFI meaning Request for Information.

I think it is fascinating to take this and reflect for a moment on the world and universe as we know it. As you proceed on this journey called life, building relationships and pursuing education or career goals to build a figurative building that brings with it fulfillment, destiny, and impact, who do you turn to when you have an RFI—a request for information? Most often, we look to seek advice from someone who holds a lot of wisdom. That would be a wise first step. Sadly, sometimes we instead turn to culture and to the other definitions those around us set for fulfillment, destiny, and impact.

The opening words of the Bible state, "In the beginning, God created the heavens and the Earth. Now Earth was formless and empty, darkness was over the surface of the deep, and the Spirit of God was hovering over the waters" (Genesis 1:1–2).

In the beginning . . . There was God. . . Before the heavens and the earth . . . God was there. . . You see, God is the maker of heaven and of Earth. . . The maker of all things seen and unseen . . . God is the Great Architect. He is the

Great Architect of the life we so desire to build that includes fulfillment, destiny, and impact.

THE REQUIREMENT OF HUMILITY

The above statement may make you shout amen or scream ouch, if I may borrow a phrase from renowned Apologist Voddie Baucham. To come under the will of this notion that God is the Great Architect requires not only faith, but humility as well.

As I reflect on this, I think of the countless debates and discussions I have had on construction sites with architects and subcontractors about the right way to go about something. Most, if not all, of these discussions required a level of compromise and a great deal of humility in order to make a decision and proceed.

I purposely began this chapter with James 1:21, which says, "Humbly accept the word God has planted in your hearts, for it has the power to save your souls." What's interesting here is that although God, the Great Architect, knows what's best for our lives, He doesn't force us to follow His vision. We can go off and build whatever building we want, no matter how destructive it is to ourselves or those around us.

With God being in and of Himself love (1 John 4:16), He freely gives us the choice to trust His blueprints for our lives. If He forced us to follow Him, would that be love? It certainly wouldn't be an expression of free will.

I also want to draw attention to the word "humbly" used in James 1:21. The original Greek word used here is prautes, which by definition means gentleness and emphasizes the divine origin of meekness. HELPS Word-Studies by Helps Ministries aids us in understanding this concept more. "For the believer, meekness begins with the Lord's inspiration and finishes by His direction and empowerment. It is a divinely balanced virtue that can only operate through faith."[36]

Faith, by biblical definition, is confidence in what we hope for and assurance about what we do not see (Hebrews 11:1). I encourage you to read further regarding Faith in Action by going and reading Hebrews Chapter Eleven.

With God's divine guidance and empowerment, we can carry out the humility required so that based on faith, we can be inspired, guided, directed, and empowered to build a life of fulfillment, destiny, and impact. It requires humility to understand that sometimes what we think is fulfilling may be completely different from what is truly fulfilling.

We may be led to reflect on the verse, "Delight yourself in the Lord, and He will give you the desires of your heart," from Psalm 37:4. God does want us to experience the desires of our heart, but sometimes it requires molding, pain, and transformation to experience the deepest desires of our heart. It is important to know that what may be fulfilling in the carnal and natural world may not be fulfilling in the spiritual being of who we are.

To truly live an inspired life, filled with fulfillment, destiny, and impact, it would be wise to draw from the wellspring

---

36 Bible Hub , s.v. "4240. prautes," accessed January 14, 2021.

of life and the Eternal Spirit as opposed to the temporary pleasures constantly working to garner our attention and satisfy our itching ears (2 Timothy 4:3).

Until we come to the realization and revelation that we were created by God for God, understanding that we are and were fearfully and wonderfully made (Psalm 139:14) with intention and with a purpose, we will spend our entire lives working to either build a life never destined for us or spend our entire lives chasing our tail and missing the divine blueprints already nestled deeply within our very being. The consequence is not only frustration that exists within us—it can also be detrimental to some of the most precious relationships we have in our lives.

WHOSE BLUEPRINTS ARE YOU BUILDING FROM?

During my last year in college, when the skyscraper I had built for myself came crumbling down, the original drawings for the skyscraper along with it were destroyed. Without much hope or direction, it wasn't until I discovered the truth of our tripartite nature that my eyes were opened to a divine and supernatural set of drawings in the Bible to start rebuilding again.

When we focus on being a dichotomy, we, in essence, merge the Spirit and Soul together as one entity, leaving us to think we are simply clumps of flesh walking around with the ability to think and feel. Some would even resort to saying we are simply just like animals.

I don't often like to use the word ignorant, but when we limit our understanding of who we are to simply having a mind and body, we are also ignorant to how God works in and through us. We are prone to missing out on His lead and the ability to rest in His joy and peace. Without understanding we are Spirit, Soul, and Body, we cannot interpret the Great Architect's blueprints when it comes to building a life complete with fulfillment, secured with destiny, and permeating with impact.

When we look at how skyscrapers are built, we are awestruck by their height, their exteriors, and even sometimes the spires that sit at their peaks. Oh, how shallow it is to look at a skyscraper this way. The buildings we look at are so much more than steel, concrete, and glass. These buildings are masterfully, intentionally, and meticulously planned out.

When Taipei 101 was completed in 2004 in Taiwan, it was the tallest building in the world for six years, standing at a height of 1,667 feet. Famous for its abilities to withstand a region known for earthquakes and typhoons, we would be limited in explaining this building's strength by only understanding the skyscraper from its exterior.

Toward the top of the building is a giant steel ball acting as a wind damper. Spanning and visible from the eighty-eighth to the ninety-second floor, this steel ball is eighteen feet in diameter and weighs over 660 metric tons.[37] When the building is impacted by wind or another type of natural phenomena that sways the building in one direction, this steel ball moves in the opposite direction to help the

---

37 "Tuned Mass Damper of Taipei 101," *Atlas Obscura*, accessed January 14, 2021.

skyscraper stabilize itself, stay grounded, and maintain its secure standing position.[38]

This is an example of resiliency at its finest, and we wouldn't know this if we didn't look to investigate how or why this building was designed this way.

The architects designed this building fearfully and wonderfully. This makes me think of another Great Architect who made a creation fearfully and wonderfully—you and me.

So, what is that steel ball residing deep within you and I under and within our very being that can help us weather the storms of life and adversity? And how does it work and why does it work in the way it does? Is your passion for life and the life you are building driven by faulty blueprints, developed by pain and infection? Or are you building a life from the Great Architect's blueprints, uncovered on the other side of a reconciled and restored passion? These blueprints are the Word of God—the Bible—and they are alive and active, able to divide the soul and spirit (Hebrews 4:12). This way our soul, our passion, can be ignited, fueled, and sustained by the Great Architect as we utilize the fire within to weather the storms of life and adversity.

Do not merely listen to the word, and so deceive yourselves. Do what it says. Anyone who listens to the word but does not do what it says is like someone who looks at his face in a mirror and, after looking at himself, goes away and

---

38   Ciaran McEneaney, "A Brief History of Taiwan's Taipei 101," *Culture Trip* (blog), January 8, 2019, accessed January 14, 2021.

immediately forgets what he looks like. But whoever looks intently into the perfect law that gives freedom, and continues in it—not forgetting what they have heard, but doing it—they will be blessed in what they do.

- JAMES 1:22–25

CHAPTER 4

THE PASSION OF
THE IMAGO DEI

———

*Then God said, "Let us make mankind in our image,
in our likeness, so that they may rule over the fish
in the sea and the birds in the sky, over the livestock
and all the wild animals, and over all the creatures
that move along the ground." So, God created
mankind in His own image, in the image of God He
created them; male and female He created them.*

- GENESIS 1:26-27

The verse above has been passionately referenced with the
Latin phrase Imago Dei, which translates to "image of God."[39]
With an eloquent pronunciation, such a truth carries with
it a key blueprint to building a life of fulfillment, destiny,
and impact.

———

39   "What Does "Imago Dei" Mean? The Image of God in the Bible,"
     Christianity.com, accessed January 14, 2021.

Going to Catholic school from kindergarten all the way through high school, I learned a lot about how all men and women are created in the image of God. But despite hearing this most of my life, I never really understood what it meant to be made and created in the image of God.

Have you ever found yourself wondering what that means?

I still ponder why it took me to get to the end of myself to get to the understanding of the term Imago Dei. I sometimes still wonder why it took complete brokenness and hopelessness to realize I was made in the image of God, by God, and for God. Sometimes a building undergoing a renovation needs to not only be fixed architecturally but also structurally at its core and foundation.

So, what does it mean to be made in the Image of God?

I'd like to address this question in two parts: first, in how we reflect God's character and likeness and secondly, in how this is expressed through our being and makeup.

As God is a tripartite being, three persons in one, we too are tripartite beings, as discussed in Chapter One, having a Spirit, Soul, and Body. In this chapter, I want to zero in on how we reflect God's character and likeness internally within our Soul through the life of Jesus Christ.

THE LIKENESS OF BEING INTELLECTUAL
Being both fully divine and fully man, Jesus often used His intellect to communicate, reason, and preach to those He came into contact with, especially when He was tempted

by the devil in the wilderness and when confronted by the religious elite of His day.

Shortly after being baptized by John the Baptist, Jesus went into the wilderness and fasted for forty days and forty nights. Toward the end of His journey, He was tempted by the devil. "If you are the Son of God, tell these stones to become bread" (Matthew 4:3). Without reservation, Jesus replied to the devil, "It is written: 'Man shall not live on bread alone, but on every word that comes from the mouth of God'" (Matthew 4:4). Here, Jesus fought off temptation utilizing scripture and truth from the Old Testament.

Many lessons can be learned from this anecdote, but one key item is that Jesus was well versed in scripture. He didn't have an iPhone in His day to quickly Google search scriptural texts. Jesus knew scripture, had it memorized, and could intellectually communicate, whether to fend off temptation, or debate with the religious elites of His day.

Like Jesus, we too are intellectual beings who have the ability to think, reason, and understand. With these abilities, we can be in a position to learn, teach, and discern where God is leading us and also how to execute the plans and missions that lie before us.

THE LIKENESS OF BEING EMOTIONAL

As we discovered in the introduction, Jesus feels. Despite being God, Jesus still felt the physical suffering as any human would during the crucifixion. He also felt the internal struggles of abandonment, rejection, and hate. He experienced fear, concern, and anxiety.

Like Jesus, we too feel. But for some reason, our culture often tells us to suppress our emotions rather than confront them. We should embrace our emotional life like Jesus, especially when it comes to painful emotions.

Suppressing emotion doesn't eliminate it. It only drives it deeper, making it harder to uncover and heal later. Jesus confronted His emotions by naming His struggles in prayer. "My Father, if all things are possible, let this cup pass from me." Jesus confronted His emotions, yet continued and persevered through them. We should process our emotions like our Creator does, naming them, confronting them, and bringing them into the sovereignty and direction of our spirit. After all, the Spirit is willing, but the flesh is weak (Matthew 26:41).

Our emotional being plays a large role in our passion. Will we let our emotions govern our passion, or will we channel our passion and govern our emotions like Jesus did in the Garden of Gethsemane on the Eve of His imminent crucifixion?

THE LIKENESS OF BEING VOLITIONAL

Decisive, assertive, and confident, Jesus was bold and intentional. Being in communion with God, Jesus brought His intellectual and emotional self under the leadership of the Spirit to make the proper choices required to carry out His destiny.

Scientists report we make an average of thirty-five thousand conscious decisions each day.[40] How many of your decisions

---

40   Frank Graff, "How Many Daily Decisions Do We Make?," *UNC-TV* (blog), February 7, 2018, accessed January 14, 2021.

each day are driven by your emotions rather than intellect and emotion under the leadership of the Holy Spirit? How often do we make decisions based on what others may think about us as opposed to where God leads us?

If Jesus was led by His emotion, He may not have proceeded forth with the imminent crucifixion, which was indeed necessary for the salvation of mankind. Jesus grounded His volition by aligning His will with the Father.

Our choices, executed through volition and discernment, have an immense role in how we steward our passion and captain our soul. We hold within ourselves the ability to choose if we will be driven by fear or guided by love.

THE FIRE WITHIN

You see, I like to imagine we have something deep within us that can help us stay grounded, firm, and secure no matter the adversity we experience in this journey called life, just like the wind damper within Taipei 101. The item in question is human passion.

Passion is the human soul on fire within us, giving us life, animation, and personality.

Many perceive the human being to simply be an animal. In fact, secular humanism would say we are simply the result of random processes, whereas Christian theism would say we are the crowning glory of the Creation of God.[41] We are not

---

41 *EnigmaChurch*, "Imago Dei: The Basis for Human Rights (Voddie Baucham)," May 20, 2009, video, 8:11.

an accident, and we are not the result of a random kaboom. There is no fuel on this planet that can ignite the passion within us like the Spirit of the living God.

Like our Living God, we are a tripartite being with a Spirit, a Soul, and a Body. Many theologians have talked about this, but for some reason it's not talked about as much in the church today and in our society, especially when it comes to modern day psychology.

Modern day psychologists often simply look at the human being and treat the symptoms and the mental health of that individual without addressing spirituality. They'll talk about it with the patient if they're open to talking about it, but they really treat the mind as its own organ.

We're broken down into three distinct components that really interact with one another. So, we are not just mind, but we are spirit, soul, and body, made in the image of God.

The body has five senses: vision, hearing, smell, taste, and touch. This is how we interact with others and how we can experience pleasure and the outside world around us.

Looking at the Soul, as discussed in Chapter Two, we have our intellect, emotion, and our will. When our thoughts and feelings intermingle in our intellect and emotion, an attitude is formed that has the ability to influence our behaviors.

So, if our attitudes influence our behaviors, how would we have control? How do we control our thoughts and feelings? It's really interesting because our soul is nestled in between our spiritual being and our body. Our soul is the mediator between the spiritual and temporal worlds. Thirty-five thousand times a day we are faced with the decision to make choices grounded in spiritual, divine truth, or feelings grounded in a compromised soul.

So again, how do we develop the attitudes and principles that will lead to the behavior we want? We accomplish this by bringing our soul into a relationship with the spirit, where it is under the sovereignty, Lordship, and leadership of the Spirit.

In a sermon, Bishop Robert Barron mentions, "If the soul is rightly ordered, it can handle anything. . . worldly success or worldly failure."[42] If we order or place our soul below our body, our soul is governed and influenced by our body. In this situation, it would be led by all the materialism in this world. We would be encouraged to live life based on impulses rather than discipline. We should seek to place our soul above our body while being guided by the Spirit. This way, it is the image of God that governs our passion instead of the image of the world.

* * *

It's for this reason I like to visualize our soul as the fire within us.

Imagine fire: first as a forest fire and secondly as it is used in sterilizing items. We can see how fire can have a dualistic

---

42 *Bishop Robert Barron*, "How to Lose Your Soul (And How to Save It) — Bishop Barron's Sunday Sermon," August 30, 2020, video, 17:09.

utilization. It can cause destruction and devastation, but it can also bring about purification.

The one difference between fire and us is that we control the fire within us. It only controls us if we allow it to. We are the stewards and caretakers of our soul. God, as we will unpack in Part Two of this book, is the perfect great physician for our souls, thus empowering the fire within us to be fueled by love rather than pain.

Imagine what fire needs. Fire needs fuel, oxygen, and heat. And just like fire requires oxygen and fuel, so too does our passion. Our soul needs healthy thoughts, healthy feelings, and healthy choices.

Imagine having this flame inside of you. Imagine your thoughts and your feelings are kicking on all cylinders. It's this passion and fire within us that will be the engine for our callings in life. Every outward behavior starts from within us.

It starts with how we think, how we feel, and how we choose. That's how we do things; we focus so much on behaviors and actions. And as an example, it is like addictive behaviors. How do we stop our poor behaviors? We do so by getting to our core and understanding how the internal attitudes within us influence our outward behaviors. We unpack this by dissecting the thoughts and feelings that are forming these ill-found attitudes. Then, by confronting our wrongful thoughts and misled feelings, we can bring them into the obedience and direction of our sovereign God.

When it comes to the fire within, I also think it's important to touch upon the impact of relationships. Our passion is impacted by relationships and the environment in a profound way. A lot of this will be discussed further in Part Two. We can't control what happens inside us, especially as it pertains to relationships, but we can control how we respond. We respond via our thoughts, feelings, and choices. We are going to be in relationships with other people, and we are going to find ourselves in adverse environments, but even if we don't have control over what's happening outside of us, we do have control of what's going on within us.

It is our responsibility and choice regarding how the passion and fire within us will lead and direct us.

We are the captains of our souls. Will we let it be led by the Spirit itself, or by culture?

What will others feel and see when they experience our passion? Will they see the passion of the Imago Dei or the passion of this fallen world?

CHAPTER 5

WHY DO WE STRUGGLE?

———

Who, being in very nature God, did not consider equality
with God something to be used to his own advantage;
rather, he made himself nothing by taking the very nature
of a servant, being made in human likeness. And being
found in appearance as a man, he humbled himself by
becoming obedient to death—even death on a cross!

- PHILIPPIANS 2:6–8

What if I told you that struggling was a good thing? For
most of high school and college, I thought it was a great
thing to struggle.

Romans 5:3-4 says, "Not only so, but we also glory in our
sufferings, because we know that suffering produces perseverance; perseverance, character; and character, hope." I clung
to this verse for most of my high school and college career
and nearly most of my young adult life. I wanted to be strong,
and I wanted to grow. But the intention of my heart was that
I wanted to grow in character and perseverance, so I could
achieve more and do more, mostly for my own personal gain.

But then came college. In college, I had an opportunity to pursue every ambition and dream I ever had. I was accomplished and enjoying life, but I faced roadblocks and challenges along the way. My last year of college was completely different from the previous years.

Beginning in Mexico alone in my hotel room, I started to ponder the questions of life while this pain was starting to take root and take a hold of me. It got even worse when I went back to college and started to wrestle with suicidal ideation. I couldn't understand why I was struggling so much. I always saw myself as a good person; I had solid morals, solid values, and always sought to love and respect others. My college experience was quite contrary to my university's party culture. I didn't think I deserved the pain and suffering because "I was a good person."

But interestingly enough, there's a C. S. Lewis quote that reads,

"We can ignore even pleasure. But pain insists upon being attended to. God whispers to us in our pleasures, speaks in our conscience, but shouts in our pains: it is His megaphone to rouse a deaf world. . . No doubt pain as God's megaphone is a terrible instrument; it may lead to final and unrepented rebellion. However, it gives the only opportunity the bad man can have for amendment. It removes the veil; it plants the flag of truth within the fortress of the rebel soul."[43]

This makes me think of the book of Job in the Bible. Job was an upright and righteous man. He was good. And he was a

---

43   "C. S. Lewis > Quotes > Quotable Quote," Goodreads, accessed January 13, 2021.

good servant of the Lord. Yet he had everything taken away from him. And the pain he endured led him all the way up to regretting he was even born (Job 3:1–3).

"Why me? I didn't deserve this suffering," Job thought.

I shared a very similar thought my last year of college. Why did I deserve this? I don't deserve this! All the things I am doing are good. I am helping people. I am involved in solid clubs. Why am I going through this?

During Job's experience, his friends came alongside and said, "You must have done something, you must have sinned because God is just, you get what you deserve." But Job continued to plead his "innocence," so much so that finally he called on God and asked Him to come and explain what was going on. In their exchange, God establishes His authority over creation and over the world and his dominance in His sovereignty. But one of the biggest things that came out of this exchange between Job and God is this question of why there is so much suffering in the world.

I think the Bible Project does a good job in summarizing God's response. The Bible Project assesses this book and says we "live in an amazing world that is not designed to prevent suffering."[44] I think it's really interesting to talk about suffering in this context. Although the world is amazing, it's not designed to prevent suffering.

But I think this is all too interesting. When I think back to the C. S. Lewis quote above regarding how God shouts in our

---

44   *BibleProject*, s.v. "Overview: Job," October 22, 2015, video, 11:00.

pains, I further reflect on a recent commencement speech given by the late Chadwick Boseman.

"Sometimes you need to feel the pain and sting of defeat to activate the real passion and purpose that God predestined inside of you," said Boseman. "God says in Jeremiah, 'I know the plans I have for you, plans to prosper you and not to harm you, plans to give you hope and a future.'"[45]

I appreciate Boseman mentioning this verse in Jeremiah shortly after his thoughts on pain because all too often, many Christians and many others interpret this verse in the book of Jeremiah as God wanting us to be prosperous and be successful. But sometimes our vision of that might be different than what the Lord envisions, and sometimes in order to walk out the purpose God has for us and the plans He has for us, we might need to go through seasons of suffering that serve as molding, growing, and discipline.

The middle of my college career in 2015 was when I initially started to have this vision for a club called Passion With Purpose. Originally it was called Passion in Action, and the idea behind this movement and behind this thought was that we could help one another uncover what we're passionate about. Then, we could empower one another by finding applications and opportunities to go apply this passion in service of others.

But after going through my own struggle and pain, the whole vision for Passion With Purpose changed, and the Lord

---

45   Tyler Burns, "Chadwick Boseman's faithful purpose showed from 'Black Panther' to his dignified death," *Religion News Service*, August 31, 2020.

completely changed it inside of me. It went from being this idea about finding passion to really living with passion and experiencing passion. Because who's to say suffering should be different from passion. As we mentioned in Chapter One, passion in and of itself means to suffer.

It's a big part of our journey in life. It shouldn't be something we ignore; it should be something we learn from and see as an opportunity to uncover the real purpose God has for our lives.

Think about the struggles we encounter as an opportunity to grow closer with God. The intimacy that is required, with God, to walk out our calling is immense; not only to hear where He's leading us, but also to learn how to lean on the Holy Spirit as he equips us to walk out our calling.

Furthermore, it's also an opportunity to relate with Christ and get closer to God through the process of sanctification. In Francis Chan's book Everlasting Marriage, he says, "Tough decisions made for God's glory produce a good and right pain, a pain that believers are meant to endure in this fallen world. It's a pain that makes us stronger, holier, more in love with God and each other. Any suffering for His sake is a constant reminder of our future where all the pain will be exchanged for glory."[46]

God freely sent His one and only son down to earth for the salvation of mankind, as we'll talk about in Part Two of this book. However, if we reflect on the life of Jesus, we would

---

46   Francis Chan and Lisa Chan, *You and Me Forever: Marriage in Light of Eternity* (San Francisco: Claire Love Publishing, 2014), 9.

see how His suffering led to the biggest impact in world history—salvation for mankind.

Sometimes God needs us to get to the end of ourselves, to see his love. Think about the times when you're at your lowest point. Who is there? Sometimes even the most important people in your life aren't there. But God's always there, simply because He resides within you if you'll let Him.

So, what is it that you may be struggling with now? You could be struggling with a breakup, depression, anxiety, or stress at work; the list goes on and on.

Life could always be a current struggle if we perceive it that way. Reflect on what God may be shouting out at you with what's going on in your life.

Maybe the pain we experience is required to identify what needs to be healed so deep within us, so we could truly step into what God's called us to do and live it out with a restored passion.

It may be easy to think that if we could just escape our struggles life would be fulfilling and easy. But what if fulfillment wasn't separation from struggle, but instead uncovering true contentment, peace, and grace amid any storm or trial, amidst any struggle?

What if the whole point of struggling is to teach us and guide us deeper into a relationship with God so we can truly know what love is and then share this love with others around us?

CHAPTER 6

WAR, WRESTLING, & PASSION

For though we live in the world, we do not wage war as the world does.

- 2 CORINTHIANS 10:3

In the present day, we may quickly associate war with sounds like "boom" or "pew pew," as bombs and bullets are projected through the air toward enemies. In the days of old, however, we probably would have associated war with sounds like grunts and "cling cling" as warriors battled and swung their swords.

From the time Cain killed Abel and unfortunately up until now with no end in sight, human civilization has always been plagued with violence and war.

As if the painful realities of the effects of violence and war aren't enough, many experience violence in action movies. I myself fall into this category as I presently reflect on Steven Spielberg's war drama, Saving Private Ryan.

We have become insensitive to the realities of violence and war to varying degrees, limiting warfare only to what happens on a battlefield as opposed to also recognizing the wars fought daily at homes, in schools, in our communities, and especially within one's soul.

How interesting is it that we do not relate the wars going on outside of us with the wars being waged within us— the war on our thoughts, emotions, and choices; the war on passion.

As discussed earlier in Part One, it is a soulical passion that is ignited, cultivated, and sustained by God's love and truth, empowering us to live out our callings and ignite passion within the souls of others around us. A soulish passion on the other hand is expired, uprooted, and drained by evil.

A soulish passion keeps us from fulfilling God's true calling on our lives and poses a threat to our passion becoming fully alive in the way God intended it to be.

As it applies to fulfillment, it is not so much what we have that dictates the measure of how fulfilling our lives are; instead, it is about what our passion is filled with and fueled by that relates to the level of fulfillment in our life.

Each day, our souls remain entangled in an eternal conflict between good and evil, a war charged with incessant wrestling for dominion over our passion.

Will our passion be cultivated by liberty in God or dominated by captivity in evil?

We often ask ourselves why evil exists and strive to rule out the participation of humans' conscience in the evil we see and especially neglect the notion that demonic spirits also play a role in the evil we partake in and witness daily.

THE ORIGINS OF GOOD VS. EVIL

In Chapter Twelve of the Book of Revelation, we are told of a war that broke out in heaven—Lucifer's rebellion against God. Before his rebellion, Lucifer was one of the highest-ranking angels, with the book of Ezekiel noting Lucifer was "anointed" and "blameless" until "unrighteousness and evil" was found in him (Ezekiel 28:14–15 AMP).[47]

Filled with pride, Lucifer sought to undermine the power of God, raising his "throne above the stars of God" and making himself "like the most high" (Isaiah 14:12–14). Lucifer didn't simply seek to be like God. He wanted to become God, ruling over creation such as the stars, noted in the verse above. Elsewhere in the scriptures, these "stars" represent other angels.[48]

This rebellion earned Lucifer a new name as the devil, namely, Satan, which is a Hebrew word for "adversary" or "opponent," because of his direct opposition to God.[49]

47 Richard Pinelli, "God vs. Satan: The Battle of the Ages," Life Hope & Truth, accessed January 27, 2021.

48 Paul Luecke and Cecil Maranville, "Are Demons Real?," Life Hope & Truth, accessed January 27, 2021.

49 Ibid.

Satan wasn't alone in his rebellion against God. In fact, one third of the angels in heaven accompanied Satan in his ploys to overtake the throne of God. As Satan was cast out of heaven and hurled down to the Earth, these angels were cast down along with him (Revelation 12). These rebel angels are known as evil spirits or demons that serve as the supernatural enemy to Christians. The enemy has one major motive: "to relentlessly oppose God and to try to thwart God's purpose for humanity."[50]

The motives of evil and the enemy continue to wage on today. Even though this war has been won due to the incarnation, crucifixion, and resurrection of Jesus Christ, the battle between God and his adversaries continues, leaving God's creation in the middle of this seemingly eternal battle.

With this in mind, the questions we must ask ourselves is how does the battle between good and evil affect us and where and how is it fought?

To address the questions above, let's consult the scriptures.

"For though we live in the world, we do not wage war as the world does. The weapons we fight with are not the weapons of the world. On the contrary, they have divine power to demolish strongholds. We demolish arguments and every pretension that sets itself up against the knowledge of God, and we take captive every thought to make it obedient to Christ."

- 2 CORINTHIANS 10:3–5

---

50   Ibid.

Watchman Nee, in his book The Spiritual Man, keenly points out the verse above divulges several things. It demonstrates the reality and real presence of a battle. It tells us where the battle is fought. It reveals the objective of the battle.[51]

SPIRITUAL WARFARE

As previously mentioned, it is easy to visualize the images of war as we are familiar with them, but when it comes to spiritual warfare, take a moment to pause and visualize what this might look like.

If you visualized something out of a horror movie, you wouldn't be alone. I never became familiar with the term spiritual warfare until several years ago. In fact, many people, including some Christians, are either void of the notion of spiritual warfare or simply ignorant of its existence and its daily impact on creation and society.[52]

Woe to us who are unaware of the spiritual struggle around us and within us. But when it comes to spiritual warfare, it isn't something out of a horror movie. This is not to say that area of evil does not exist, but if we preoccupy our minds with this understanding of spiritual warfare, we would be blinded to the actual struggles going on within.

To better understand what spiritual warfare is, think of it as an information war between two parties where one is fact while the other is folly; where one is truth, and the other is heresy.

---

51 Nee, *The Spiritual Man*, 8.

52 Ibid., 55.

The book of Ephesians notes:

"For we do not wrestle against flesh and blood, but against the rulers, against the authorities, against the cosmic powers over this present darkness, against the spiritual forces of evil in the heavenly places."

- EPHESIANS 6:12, ESV

Apologist Voddie Baucham elaborates on the above verse that we are, in actuality, at war with ideas that stand in opposition to the truth of the Gospel.[53] The war between good and evil is truly the war on Truth.

To some, this may not appear as a large ordeal, but this is something we should not only concern ourselves with, but also engage on the offensive for.

Truth in God's eyes goes beyond scientific fact, reason, and evidentiary standards. Truth was, truth is, and truth always will be. In fact, Jesus tells us the truth sets us free (John 8:32).

When we embark on our personal quests for meaning, significance, and purpose, we are truly seeking after Truth.

Truth is the path to salvation. Truth is the Great Architect's blueprints outlining the drawings to build a life of fulfillment, destiny, and impact.

---

53 *The Gospel of Christ*, "We Must Fight - Voddie Baucham | 01-16-2021," January 17, 2021, video, 35:55.

For as long as the enemy clouds the minds of Christ's followers, disrupting truth in believers, the destiny laid before us will appear as faded drawings.

As discussed throughout Part One of this book, the intellect, or mind, is the gateway to future decisions and behaviors. For this reason, spiritual warfare is fought within the battlefield of the mind.

THE BATTLEFIELD OF THE MIND

One of the most important principles in Part One is understanding the distinction among Spirit, Soul, and Body, especially the distinction between spirit and soul. Such an applicable understanding is necessary when it comes to the battlefield of the mind.

The function of the mind is understanding, while the function of intuition is knowing. The goal of the mind is to understand thoughts through rationalization, while the goal of intuition is to spiritually discern the truth, that is, the thoughts of the Holy Spirit which are then communicated down to one's soul in the mind, eventually leading an individual to make a decision.[54]

Remember, the soul is the mediator between the spiritual and natural world, the spiritual world being what is discerned and communicated from our heavenly Father and the natural world being what is communicated through the body's five senses and the soul's emotions and desires.

---

54   Nee, *The Spiritual Man*, 72–75.

Further clarifying, our intellect, the mind, processes information from several sources through two mediums. The mediums are the spiritual realm and the natural realm. The three sources of information are God, the enemy (devil), and the self. God communicates to us through the Spirit while the enemy and the self communicate to us from the outside in.[55]

A good way to digest this is by compartmentalizing and defining the inner man and the outward man. The inner man is composed of the spirit, while the outward man is composed of the soul and body. Yes, the soul is the mediator between the Spirit and the Body, but because of man's fallen nature, our broken souls (our mind or emotion) are a part of the outward man.[56] This is also spelled out in Romans 8:7: "The mind governed by the flesh is hostile to God; it does not submit to God's law, nor can it do so."

When it comes to building a life of fulfillment, destiny, and impact and especially when it comes to discerning God's will for our lives and experiencing the fruits and empowerment of the Holy Spirit, how difficult it is for our minds to truly uncover and dissect truth from falsehood and direction from distraction.

Putting demonic possessions aside, the devil mostly attacks Christians from the outside in.[57] These attacks are described as fiery arrows in Ephesians 6:16 and are described as "arguments" in 2 Corinthians 10:5 (NIV translation). The original

---

55   Ibid., 72.

56   Ibid.

57   Ibid.

word for argument used in the scriptures is the Greek word, logismos, which is literally a reasoning or thought.[58]

The enemy implies and utilizes thoughts to influence and attack the mind of believers. Difficult to discern, these spiritual attacks are difficult to differentiate from our own personal thoughts.

THE ENEMY'S OBJECTIVE

As mentioned above, the enemy seeks "to relentlessly oppose God and to try to thwart God's purpose for humanity." One of the best ways to do this is by manifesting evil in the world through the physical actions of people.

With our thoughts, feelings, and attitudes leading to behaviors, the devil literally seeks to hijack and influence our minds for his motives. These motives have detrimental effects on us and unfortunately, on those closest to us.

The enemy's attacks carry with them a dualistic blow. They undermine the function of our intellect by way of distraction and false leading with lies and deception. Even worse, they suppress and crush our spirit—not the spirit of morale as the world defines spirit, but the Spirit of Truth, God's still, small voice within us that gently leads us into His callings on our lives.

Proverbs 18:14 reads, "The human spirit can endure in sickness, but a crushed spirit who can bear?"

---

58   Bible Hub, s.v. "3053. logismos," accessed January 27, 2021.

By crushing the spirit of a person through mind pollution and overrunning the mind with countless thoughts, the enemy thereby quenches the spirit. The enemy seeks to do this by filling one's mind "with various wandering thoughts. [The Devil] intends to confuse one's spiritual awareness by these sensations and thoughts. While confused, God's children are incompetent to distinguish what is of the spirit and what emanates from the soul."[59]

In doing so, the enemy works to get Christians to live a soul-ish life—a life lived by feeling and emotion rather than by truth and conviction. If the devil can get individuals to live based on feelings, he can control people by ways of bondage through pain.

We will uncover this more in Part Two, but it is important to note the enemy's primary objective is to control you by crushing your spirit and by utilizing your emotions, your passion, against you. It's all about his gain at your expense.

Contrary to this, God's plan for you is your gain at His expense. What a testimony of unconditional love that flows ever so freely to our spirits, guiding us in the ways of the Lord.

Where the Spirit of the Lord is there is freedom (2 Corinthians 3:17). Where the spirit of the enemy is there is bondage, "for 'people are slaves to whatever has mastered them'" (2 Peter 2:19).

The enemy wants you to operate out of the false self, while your Heavenly Creator desires for you to operate out of

---

59   Nee, *The Spiritual Man*, 136.

your true self. Woe to us who make countless decisions each and every day operating from a place of pain and the false self as opposed to operating from a place of truth, our true self, who God so fearfully and wonderfully made (Psalm 139:14).

The Holy Spirit moves people themselves to work, never setting aside man's personality; the evil spirit demands men to be entirely inactive so that he may work in their place, reducing man's spirit to a robot.

- WATCHMAN NEE[60]

As pointed out above, the enemy can thwart God's purpose in our lives by influencing us to pursue paths contrary to God's plans for our lives, or he can undermine God's plan for our lives by confusing us to the point where we become idle, passive, or inactive. The fire of passion isn't meant to stay still and illuminate a limited radius. The fire of passion is meant to impart love, care, faith, grace, and mercy and serve as the engine that executes our purpose.

Once we acknowledge the spiritual conflict we are in, we can put on the full Armor of God, take up arms, and take the fight to the enemy.

FROM SOLDIER TO WARRIOR

One of the biggest distinctions between a soldier and a warrior is that one battles while the other, though fully trained

---

60   Ibid., 63

and prepared, is on standby as if on the sidelines of the field of battle.

While our loving Creator instituted mercy and the principles of this Universe, the enemy plays by no rules and is both merciless and relentless. Simply speaking, the enemy wants to completely thwart the plans of God and His plans for our lives by severing our relationship with God.

Just as the serpent utilized lies and deception in the temptation, or attack, on Adam and Eve, so too does the enemy ever incessantly convolute our thoughts with cunning lies and more specifically, twisted truth (see 2 Corinthians 11). The devil applied the tactic of truth twisting when tempting Jesus after He fasted in the wilderness, by attempting to twist the Scriptures against Jesus to get Him to succumb to temptation. How Jesus responded to this attack is a great model of how we should fend off the enemy.

A warrior in battle does not only fight on the offensive, but also fights on the defensive as well. In the book of Jude, we are urged to "contend for the faith" (NIV). The word contend here comes from the Greek word epagonizomai, which literally means "to wrestle."[61]

Now I know you are tempted to think about the WWE and the wrestling entertainment industry when we think of the word wrestling, but put that thought aside for a moment. I'd like for you to reflect on collegiate wrestling.

---

61 *The Gospel of Christ*, "We Must Fight - Voddie Baucham | 01-16-2021," January 17, 2021, video, 35:55.

When wrestlers are on the mat, we can typically observe three techniques: offensiveness, defensiveness, and the infamous riding time. Riding time in wrestling is the instance where one opponent with the advantageous position holds the opponent in the disadvantaged position firm.

Now for the opponent in the disadvantaged position, it may seem like an okay place to be in. He isn't getting pinned and succumbing to pain, but he is still losing. The opponent in the advantaged position gains points in correlation with the amount of time he remains in position.

With this in mind, I want you to visualize the enemy relentlessly tempting your mind with lies and lofty ideas. Now visualize it becoming unbearable to the point where you just want to cover your head and scream out, hoping it will all be over soon. Such a way of wrestling will never lead to victory.

We must remain confident in the truth that the same Holy Spirit that raised Jesus Christ from the dead resides within you and within me (Romans 8:11).

By the power of His Spirit, we must engage in the fight both offensively and defensively. Just as wrestlers will use the momentum of their opponent to transition from a defensive position to an offensive position, so too must we engage the enemy.

Despite thousands of years in warfare history, there remains yet just one weapon that delivers both an offensive and defensive strike simultaneously. This is the sword.

Interestingly enough the scriptures point out the below as it pertains to the full Armor of God:

"Finally, be strong in the Lord and His mighty power. Put on the full armor of God, so that you can take your stand against the devil's schemes. For our struggle is not against flesh and blood, but against the rulers, against the authorities, against the powers of this dark world and against the spiritual forces of evil in the heavenly realms. Therefore put on the full armor of God, so that when the day of evil comes, you may be able to stand your ground, and after you have done everything, to stand. Stand firm then, with the belt of truth buckled around your waist, with the breastplate of righteousness in place, and with your feet fitted with the readiness that comes from the Gospel of peace. In addition to all this take up the shield of faith, with which you can extinguish all the flaming arrows of the evil one. Take the helmet of salvation and the sword of the Spirit, which is the word of God."

- EPHESIANS 6:10-17

Now though this chapter is dense, must I remind you this book is not solely about Spiritual Warfare. Though this principle is incredibly important to this book and to Truth as believers, we will save dissecting the entire passage above for another day.

Within the context of our present discussion, the key phrase I'd like to discuss more from the verse above is the sword of the Spirit, which is the word of God. As briefly mentioned above, the sword delivers both offensive and defensive blows.

Jesus in his bout with the Devil in Matthew, Chapter Four, models the use of Scriptures as a weapon of sword in a way that we must pay attention to and model ourselves. Each time the devil tempted Jesus with twisted truth, Jesus assertively responded with Truth, the written Word of God. This encounter lasted three exchanges until the Devil finally left Jesus as a result of His faithful application of truth to tear down lies.

I must make note that if even the Son of Man needed several strikes of the sword for the enemy to retreat, should we think we can fend off the enemy with simply one strike or even worse, by laying down our swords and crouching, covering our heads?

Certainly not! We are charged in the scriptures to test each spirit or thought that infiltrates our mind and most assertively and aggressively wrestle for the Truth:

Do not quench the Spirit. Do not treat prophecies
with contempt but test them all; hold on to
what is good, reject every kind of evil.
- 1 THESSALONIANS 5:19-22

Beloved, do not believe every spirit, but test the spirits
to see whether they are from God, for many false
prophets have gone out into the world. By this you
know the Spirit of God: every spirit that confesses that
Jesus Christ has come in the flesh is from God, and
every spirit that does not confess Jesus is not from

God. This is the spirit of the antichrist, which you
heard was coming and now is in the world already.

Exercising the charge above is how we truly fend off the enemy. As articulated in 2 Corinthians 10:5, "We demolish arguments and every pretension that sets itself up against the knowledge of God, and we take captive every thought to make it obedient to Christ."

THE WAR ON PASSION

All throughout Part One of this book, we have redefined and referred to passion as an experience, something that we build, and finally something that is cultivated, fostered, and malleable.

As we continue to understand passion as a mechanism to carry out God's plan for our lives, we will continue to realize the importance of the role it plays in living out God's will for our lives.

My heart earnestly desires for you to come to the realization that a life filled with fulfillment, destiny, and impact will often not look like how society and culture defines these things.

The War on Passion is just one aspect of building a life of ful-fillment, but as we ignite and protect our passion by inspiring our souls with the truth of the Great Architect, as opposed to filling our souls with the filthy lies of this world, we will begin to live a life inspired by the Great Architect and enjoy the beauty of this world's relationships and creations in the way our Heavenly Father so destined us to live it.

Let God inspire your passion so the gifts within you can come to complete fullness and impact the lives of others around you.

Remember, God wants you to utilize your passion to exercise and execute a plan that serves Him and blesses you, while the enemy seeks to rob you of your personality, take you hostage, and use your passion for his motives, which often result in pain and destruction.

With all this said, I leave you with this question as you reflect on this chapter. Is God using your passion for you? Or is the enemy using your passion against you?

CHAPTER 7

FULFILLMENT – WINNING THE WAR ON PASSION

———

By the grace God has given me, I laid a foundation as a wise builder, and someone else is building on it. But each one should build with care. For no one can lay any foundation other than the one already laid, which is Jesus Christ. If anyone builds on this foundation using gold, silver, costly stones, wood, hay or straw, their work will be shown for what it is, because the Day will bring it to light. It will be revealed with fire, and the fire will test the quality of each person's work. If what has been built survives, the builder will receive a reward. If it is burned up, the builder will suffer loss but yet will be saved—even though only as one escaping through the flames.

- 1 CORINTHIANS 3:10-15

Fulfillment usually encompasses significance, meaning, purpose, destiny, and impact. These are all deep needs of the soul and things we all seek and pursue, yet many feel as though we come up short in seeking out this endeavor.

Despite the realization that fulfillment is about the journey and not the destination, as demonstrated in Ralph Waldo Emerson's famous quote, "Life is a journey, not a destination," it can sometimes still be a challenge to find fulfillment in the present and avoid associating fulfillment with a destination or a dream being reached.[62]

I know in my life, I have been guilty of both and in some ways still battle to find fulfillment in the present for practical reasons, like many other people.

But let's begin with the principle that fulfillment in life is dependent upon the moment rather than upon accomplishing a dream we may have set for ourselves far off in the distance.

As previously mentioned, my biggest dream was to build skyscrapers around the world. I spent my childhood and teen years venturing into Manhattan and walking around lower Manhattan being struck by awe and wonder at the marvel, beauty, and resilience of the towers that rose around me, especially the construction of the New World Trade Center.

From eighth grade on, I made it my life goal to go out and build skyscrapers around the world—from writing

---

62 "Ralph Waldo Emerson > Quotes > Quotable Quote," Goodreads, accessed January 13, 2021.

letters to some of the world's largest and most renowned architectural and engineering firms, including SOM and WSP Structural Engineering, to pulling all-nighter after all-nighter in college.

After three consecutive summer internships with my dream construction company, I was given the opportunity to intern internationally in Mexico City and better yet, the project I would proceed to work on was a skyscraper.

After this experience, I was given the opportunity to begin my career with my dream company's international group. In spite of accomplishing a major dream I had set for myself at an early age, there was one major piece missing.

Fulfillment.

It was nowhere to be found, and like a deck of cards comes crumbling down at a puff of air, so too did my life come crumbling down.

The unmet fulfillment expectation of my dream coupled with other life experiences going on at age twenty-two played a monumental role in the depression I encountered during my last year of college and as I began my career.

You see, I fell into the fulfillment trap. I made my life all about the dream. I built up within my mind this notion that in order to be significant, have meaning, and have worth, I needed to accomplish the dream of constructing buildings around the world. I thought an accomplishment would inspire people more than simply being kind, loving, and authentic.

In a way, my dream was fueled by a *soulish passion* and thus became an idol. When a dream becomes an idol, it robs you of the moment and especially the precious moments with the loved ones around you.

This is so because dreams cause us to be futuristic, making the present moment about the dream ahead of us rather than what we immediately have now.

Author, pastor, and leadership expert John C. Maxwell exclaims, "I love the day and what I can do now more than I love the dream and what I can do someday."[63]

Many would agree with Dr. Maxwell, and in fact, many would agree that a major key to fulfillment is being content in the moment and maximizing presence.

Even mainstream culture has echoed the values of mindfulness and presence in recent years. In the last two decades alone, mindfulness journal publications increased 22,133 percent. Yes. That is a comma and not a period—**twenty-two thousand** percent![64]

The sad fact is mindfulness has become a buzzword and hip way to communicate you're in touch with reality.

The issue with mindfulness is it encourages one to become present but doesn't empower one to confront the deep issues

63   *Quang Vu*, "Question 9 Fulfillment," November 11, 2018, video, 17:02.

64   Drake Baer, "How Mindfulness Went from Fringe To Mainstream," Thrive Global, accessed February 2, 2021.

and insecurities that may be plaguing them from within. Rather than confronting the soul, mindfulness focuses more attention on the body. *Psychology Today* notes mindfulness also includes an increased attention to nutrition, exercise, breathing, relationships, and fitness.[65]

Let me be clear: I am not ruling out the tremendous benefit nutrition and exercise has on one's health and wellness, especially not how it can and will lead to a healthier lifestyle. But we must be careful in making fulfillment dependent on one's health. It goes deeper than that.

Fulfillment is peace and contentment within oneself regardless of the circumstances around us **and** also within us, including health.

Healthy eating and fitness will not heal the soul from painful past traumas that may be rising up and waging war on one's soul, robbing it of the moment. Furthermore, if we were to make fulfillment about health, then how would we explain fulfillment to someone with a terminal illness or who fights a chronic disease?

You would be surprised to know some who face this reality may in actuality experience more fulfillment than someone who is "living large" and has everything according to the standards set forth by the world.

Such a person has won the war on passion.

---

65   Frank John Ninivaggi, "Why Has Mindfulness Become So Popular?," *Psychology Today*, accessed February 2, 2021.

I love John Maxwell's quote above. I might even have to make it the background on my phone for a period of time to keep me grounded and focused.

But in reality, life is tough. There is no escaping the real adversities we encounter. Things will happen to us, and the impacts they imprint on our soul can last forever.

Is it easy to live in the moment when your parents get divorced? Is it easy to live in the moment when a loved one dies? Is it easy to live in the moment when you have thoughts of suicide without conscious reasons why? Is it easy to be in the moment when people you care about bully you? Is it easy to live in the moment when you have a boss who despises your values and treats you like a piece of wood? Is it easy to live in the moment when someone lies or cheats you? Is it easy to live in the moment when you receive a terminal health diagnosis?

We need to stop building a life of fulfillment according to the blueprints of this fallen and ruthless society overtaken by pride and greed.

Fulfillment is not about what we have—it is about *who* we have. It's about Jesus. It's about building a life inspired by the Great Architect who commands us to love God and through this realized love, love people unconditionally without reservation.

The key to passion is a healthy soul. The key to fulfillment is a healthy Spirit, Soul, and Body.

Only one caretaker exists for all three of these faculties: God. As we will discuss throughout the rest of this book, when we build a relationship with God outside the confines of religious rituals, when God the Father inspires our mind, when Jesus the Son encourages our emotion, or when the Holy Spirit empowers our will, it is then when we truly experience fulfillment.

This is how we fill our souls with the love of Christ. For fulfillment is not about being filled with pride and accomplishment. Instead, fulfillment is about being filled with Christ.

So, I ask you. Who owns your heart? Who cares for your soul and shepherds you? Who ignites, fuels, and sustains the passion within you?

Is it the world or enemy who uses your passion against you or is it the lamb of God?

Confronting the pain of the present which seeks to rob us of the moment will be a challenge we face for the rest of our lives. But because of God's grace and goodness, we have eternal access to fill our souls with the fruits of the same Spirit that raised Christ from the dead.

When we rest in Jesus, our savior, our sanctifier, our healer, our redeemer, our deliverer, the prince of peace and coming king, it is here that we can take the fight to the devil.

This way, no matter what is going on around us or within us, we can bring Jesus to the fight along with us and stand our ground in the moment, channeling our passion to experience fulfillment in the moment and, as a result, apply our passion in a way that can allow God to work through us and in us as He desires to.

* * *

On the eve of His crucifixion, enduring, and passion, a journey which would lead to salvation for mankind, Jesus sought to be alone with the Father.

Jesus expressed his sorrow, anxiety, and pain. Jesus entered the throne room of the Father. And in this instance, he created an opportunity for the Spirit of God to fall afresh on Him to inspire, encourage, and empower Jesus within the soul to take on the wrestling and war within.

Sometimes in this life, our view of what fulfillment is might be completely contrary to that of God.

Building a life of fulfillment and winning the war on passion requires us to care about God's will over our own desires.

Let us always keep Jesus—the way of fulfillment, the truth of destiny, and the life of impact—as the author and caretaker of our passion. May we take up our cross daily, and when our war on passion gets to the point where we question God and His plan, may we respond as Jesus did in the garden and say, "Yet not my will, but yours be done."

For it is when we build a life inspired by the Great Architect that we can truly comprehend where God is leading us and guiding us toward.

PART TWO

DESTINY

*BUILDING A LIFE ENCOURAGED
BY THE GREAT PHYSICIAN*

Let us look inward and invite Jesus, the Great
Physician, into our hearts so He can reveal to
us our destiny and callings in life.

CHAPTER 8

JOBS, CAREERS, CALLINGS & PURPOSE

———

Whatever you do, work at it with all your heart, as working for the Lord, not for human masters, since you know that you will receive an inheritance from the Lord as a reward. It is the Lord Christ you are serving.

- COLOSSIANS 3:23–24

Within all of us lies this strong desire to feel a sense of significance, worth, and especially purpose. When searching for books on Amazon on "purpose," over sixty thousand results show up. Despite so many perspectives and so-called solutions when it comes to uncovering a life of purpose, why do so many still find themselves pondering their purpose and feeling dissatisfied with their life?

I think it may be that we are asking the wrong question. We want purpose because we want significance, value, worth, and meaning. I think it is so easy to confuse purpose with activities because so many activities like jobs, careers, and especially callings do give us a sense of purpose.

But what if the purpose we seek is truly found first in a relationship as opposed to an activity? Let's take jobs and careers for example. People who love their jobs and careers and feel a sense of purpose often attribute it to the people they work with—not always, but often. Many others just simply love the activities they do, but is there a difference between purpose and enjoyment?

If we truly want to live a life of purpose, it is important to realize that while enjoyment may be an experience we feel internally, making it about us, purpose is about others and relationships, and the mutual impact shared in those encounters.

In his book, Emotionally Healthy Spirituality, Pete Scazzero talks about the temptations we have toward a false self or toward false identities. These false identities are rooted in emotional woundedness and pain. Some people can spend so much of their life searching to fill the voids in their heart with these false identities. Pete Scazzero brilliantly combines and categorizes these false identities into three groups: Performance-based (I am What I Do), Possession (I am What I Have), and Popularity (I Am What Others Think).[66]

When the building I had built for myself collapsed during my final year of college, the above three false identities had been

66 Peter Scazzero, *Emotionally Healthy Spirituality: It's Impossible to be Spiritually Mature While Remaining Emotionally Immature, Updated Edition* (Grand Rapids: Zondervan, 2017), 49–52.

fueling my drive, passion, and purpose. I put all of my worth into the impact I could make. I put all of my worth into the accomplishments I had. I put all of my worth into what others thought of me. In fact, I was known for my passion for life.

Despite reaching the peak of performance, possession, and popularity, I fell into a battle with unhappiness and further depression that wrecked me. It was like my life was experiencing an earthquake.

The foundation of my life was rooted in pain and the inequities of the past. My foundation was shallow and filled with voids. I tried to fill those voids with performance, possession, and popularity, but when we try to fill the voids within us with false identities, they never truly satisfy our needs.

While jobs and careers are great avenues to feed our false identities, callings can also be utilized to meet the needs and desires of a false self, depending on where the calling comes from.

From a secular viewpoint, Forbes defines a calling as the "alignment between vocation and one's identity . . . where there is a personal and emotional connection to the work."[67] With this definition, we merely breach the surface of what a calling truly is and where it comes from.

Expert of leadership and renowned Author John C. Maxwell defines calling as "purpose on steroids" in his Leadership

---

67 Melody Wilding, "Do You Have a Job, Career or Calling? The Difference Matters," *Forbes*, April 23, 2018.

Podcast episode on Calling and Purpose. Maxwell goes on to say, "Remember this, God created you with your purpose and with that purpose, He gave you strengths and gifts to fulfill it."[68]

Pastor and New York Times best-selling author Craig Groeschel offers another alternative definition to callings in his book Chazown. Groeschel notes in his book the word vision that appears in Old Testament scriptures comes from the Hebrew word, chazown, which means "dream," "revelation," or "vision."[69]

Interestingly enough, God often communicated with many people throughout scripture with dreams and visions when He called them or lead them to something.

To aid readers in discerning their "chazown," or calling, Groeschel presents what he identifies as the "Three-Part Harmony" in his book, which is composed of three elements: Core Values, Spiritual Gifts, and Past Experiences. Where the three intersect is where our chazown lies.[70]

Reflection on our values, spiritual gifting, and past experiences requires more than simple personal reflection. It

---

68 John Maxwell and Mark Cole, "Calling and Purpose," September 1, 2020, in *The John Maxwell Leadership Podcast*, produced by John C. Maxwell, podcast, MP3 audio, 23:14.

69 Craig Groeschel, *Chazown: Discover and Pursue God's Purpose for Your Life - Revised and Updated Edition* (United States: Multnomah - The Crown Publishing Group, 2017), 8-9.

70 Craig Groeschel, *Chazown: Discover and Pursue God's Purpose for Your Life - Revised and Updated Edition* (United States: Multnomah - The Crown Publishing Group, 2017), 63–64.

requires a journey with Jesus alongside us as we navigate the deeper areas of our being while we grow stronger in our relationship with Him.

ANSWERING THE CALL

It seems like telemarketers are calling my phone more and more recently. Whenever I see random numbers on my phone, even if it is a familiar area code, I ignore the call, silence it, and sometimes in frustration throw my phone across the room. Oh, how much more likely we are to answer the phone when we know who is on the other side.

The fascinating thing when it comes to callings from a Christian theism perspective is that our callings come from God. Equipped with spiritual gifts, it is God who calls on us to walk them out and live out our callings. But if we truly want to know what our calling is, it may require us to know who is calling us. It may require us to know who Jesus is.

How quickly would you answer the phone if the caller ID said "Jesus?" How often do our "phones" ring containing the calling of our life, but because we lack the personal relationship, we either ignore or miss the call?

This is intentionally so. The calling you and I have requires much more beyond commitment and perseverance. In fact, we cannot truly live out our callings with a passion fueled by our own strength. We need to be fueled by a supernatural and spirit-filled passion. Such a passion can be only built upon that which is Jesus Christ.

*For no one can lay any foundation other than
the one already laid, which is Jesus Christ.*

- 1 CORINTHIANS 3:11

*The stone which the builders rejected Has
become the chief cornerstone.*

- PSALM 118:22

*Thus, the Lord God says, "Behold, I lay in Zion a stone
for a foundation, a tried stone, a precious cornerstone, a
sure foundation; whoever believes will not act hastily.*

- ISAIAH 28:16

*Now, therefore, you are no longer strangers and
foreigners, but fellow citizens with the saints and
members of the household of God, having been built
on the foundation of the apostles and prophets, Jesus
Christ Himself being the chief cornerstone, in whom the
whole building, being fitted together, grows into a holy
temple in the Lord, in whom you also are being built
together for a dwelling place of God in the Spirit."*

- EPHESIANS 2:19–22

When we come into relationship with Jesus, not only do we
experience the infilling of the Holy Spirit as discussed in Part
One; our eyes are also opened to receive and understand the
calling God has placed on our lives. As Christians, we are
called to disciple, minister to others around us, and share the

gospel with others. Those are our given callings as believers. But along with that and our spiritual gifts is a call.

One important thing to consider, however, is that many things in our lives can distract us from our true callings. Christian psychologist Dominic Herbst, who also happens to be a dear mentor of mine, has done a teaching that discusses how "the good thing isn't always the God thing." Often enough our lives, along with the plans and visions we set for ourselves, lack in comparison to what God has for us.

Romans 12:2 says, "Do not conform to the pattern of this world, but be transformed by the renewing of your mind. Then you will be able to test and approve what God's will is—his good, pleasing and perfect will."

Through a personal relationship with Christ, we welcome into our spirits the gift of the Holy Spirit who sanctifies our intuition, which guides our process in the renewing of our mind.

Whatever opportunities come our way in this life, we must be always discerning, testing, and approving of what is from the Lord, especially as it pertains to the callings on our lives.

Jesus doesn't drive us into our calling. He gently leads us and guides us, ensuring it is us exercising the gift of free will to trust Him, follow Him, and answer His call on our life.

We also must remain humble and always stay grounded in relationship with God. It is not our calling that gives us purpose. It is our relationship with God that gives us purpose first and foremost. The Lord may giveth and taketh (Job 1:21) as it pertains to the people, relationships, and activities in our lives, but once we enter into relationship with Him, it's completely up to us if we want to remain under and in His divine truth, divine love, and divine guidance.

As the Father has loved me, so have I
*loved you. Now **remain** in my love.*

- JOHN 15:9

CHAPTER 9

PURPOSE VS. DESTINY

———

And we know that God causes everything to work
together for the good of those who love God and
are called according to his purpose for them.

- ROMANS 8:28

In Holocaust survivor Viktor Frankl's book, Man's Search for Meaning, he notes, "Man's search for meaning is the primary motivation in his life and not a secondary rationalization of instinctual drives."[71]

As discussed in Part One, one of our soul's biggest needs is meaning and significance. Our souls desire to be valued by others and to have a sense of worth as we seek to make a difference.

All of our basic physiological needs can be in abundance, but our soul will always crave meaning.

---

71 "Dennis Prager: Man's Search for Meaning by Viktor Frankl," Prager University, accessed February 2, 2021.

Typical words that go along with the pursuit of meaning and significance include purpose and destiny. Purpose and destiny are both two very powerful but distinct words, and we utilize each interchangeably, not realizing the true differences between them.

Understanding the difference between purpose and destiny is paramount to building a life of destiny.

Purpose originally stems from the Greek word *pauein*, which means "to stop or to cease," while destiny comes from the Latin word *destinare*, which means to "make firm, or establish."[72]

One of these words refers to a moment set in a particular time and space while the other implies a moment set before, during, and after in time and space. In other words, by being eternal, it is outside of time and space.

We seek to live purposeful lives by seeking after destiny, not realizing that destiny is an eternal destination, based on establishment, while purpose consists of critical moments along the way. Think of destiny as the destination set before us that was, is, and always will be. We will get to this more later.

But if we seek to live purposeful lives by pursuing destiny, we may miss out on the opportunities to live purposeful lives throughout our life journey.

---

72 "purpose (n.)," Online Etymology Dictionary, accessed February 2, 2021; "destiny (n.)," Online Etymology Dictionary, accessed February 2, 2021.

You see, our purpose isn't a one-time thing. It's the very next thing, as coined in Casting Crowns's 2016 album name. When we begin to see our purpose as something present and in the moment as opposed to an impact far off in the distance, we will see opportunities to have a purpose and opportunities to inspire, encourage, or empower someone. Whether listening to a friend vent or giving comforting words to a complete stranger, it is inspiring, encouraging, and empowering others around us that leads to a purposeful life.

Even if we look at it from an operational or work standpoint, the same truth applies. It may be easy to get caught up in the moment thinking the action itself is purposeful, but the real purpose taking place is the impact, good, or service you are providing.

I intentionally made the message of differentiating purpose and destiny as its own chapter because this is a principle I don't want you to miss out on.

God has called each of us to have a purpose. But sometimes the purpose he has intended for us to make is not the purpose we would have pursued ourselves.

There comes a point to purposeful living where we must humble ourselves before the Lord and have purpose where he has planted us.

When I began my career, I was assigned to a project in the Pocono Mountains in Eastern Pennsylvania. To be honest, it was the last place I wanted to go or start my career. Coming off a difficult final year of college, I intended to start my career in Philadelphia surrounded by friends in a familiar environment to begin the process of building myself back up from the season of depression I walked through in college.

But just a few weeks before starting my career, I was assigned to a large project in the Pocono Mountains. It was an incredible opportunity, but it also seemed completely contrary to what I thought I needed or wanted to do.

Huffing and puffing as I drove my Jeep to the Poconos to begin my career with reluctance, never would I have imagined how God would have used that experience like He did to complete a mission within me. I am convinced this wouldn't have happened any other way. There's more to this, but this will be tabled for another book.

I started on the project as a field engineer, and in this role, it was my responsibility to run around the project and chase subcontractors to make sure they delivered their contract responsibilities in a way that upheld safety, quality, and the project's schedule.

One of the subcontractors I managed was the fire protection subcontractor. To this day, one of my favorite parts about construction is the relationships you forge and the people you meet on the job.

The construction industry can be a grind at times. It is a fast-paced environment that can cause a lot of pent-up emotions and stress. The industry is diverse in the sense that you can have someone on a project site who graduated with a high school diploma all the way up to someone who has a PhD or is a CEO of a company.

All individuals have a different story, and each worker brings to the project what's going on within them, including personal challenges at home.

I'll never forget Sprinkler Fitter Bob. Bob was a middle-aged journeyman sprinkler fitter with a short salt-and-pepper goatee.

Bob spent most of the day in a mechanical lift hanging sprinklers that ranged from large six-inch wide pipes to small two-inch pipes. Bob wasn't a fan of wearing his safety glasses and at times would "forget" to wear his safety harness while within the lift. This was an OSHA standard and job-site requirement.

Bob was a little high strung. He didn't like to be told what to do, especially by a twenty-three year old kid who just started in the business with brand new work boots and clean jeans.

I didn't want to seem like the "safety police" and wanted to demonstrate the policy I was enforcing was well intentioned and grounded in my concern for Bob's safety.

In order to communicate these intentions with Bob, I started to build a relationship with him. I started to ask him about how he got into the trade, and these conversations led us to talking about his kids and family life.

It didn't take long until he started to open up about a painful divorce he was going through with his wife and how his wife was using manipulation and deceit to turn his own kids against him and get them on her side.

Of course, there's two sides to every story, but the fact of the matter was that Bob was truly dealing with some emotional conflicts. Imagine working with your hands and feet to provide for a family that is crumbling apart while your spouse is making you out to be the bad guy and rejecting you.

My heart broke for Bob, and I think he could tell I genuinely cared about what was going on in his life. Through this barrier breaking down, not only did Bob begin to start upholding the safety policies, but we began to have deeper conversations, especially conversations on faith and what I believed in.

For the duration of the time we worked together, he asked many questions, and I did my best to honestly answer them and provide encouragement for him every time I could.

I think it can be easy for us to think we can escape problems from home by delving into our work and studies as a distraction, but the fact of the matter is that what's in us travels with us and has the chance to adversely affect the way we work and behave.

Who knows; maybe Bob could have had an accident one day on site, distracted by the problems going on at home. Thankfully this never happened and looking back now, I'm grateful to have been managing the fire protection company because I was able to meet Bob and hopefully be a glimmer of hope.

When I reflect back on my time in the Poconos, I think sometimes about whether God placed me in the Poconos for almost two years simply to have that daily exchange with Bob. I may not get a clear answer from God regarding this, and that's the thing. Most of the moments in our life where we have the biggest impact and purpose are the moments we never planned for.

The path opens up the door for purpose. And when our path is ordered by God and we are obedient, He will create divine appointments among many other opportunities to have a purpose beyond measure.

*"In their hearts humans plan their course, but
the Lord establishes their steps."*

- PROVERBS 16:9 (NIV)

It is important to humble ourselves before the Lord and the Great Architect for our lives and trust He knows where and how to use us to have the biggest purpose.

Our purpose is innumerable both over the course of our life and in the present. It is our destiny that is instead established.

The one thing purpose and destiny do have in common is that they are both relationship dependent. As demonstrated, purpose impacts the lives of others at every opportunity. Purpose is about others, not simply us. In the Western world and in America, it is easy to make purpose about ourselves and our happiness, but when we do this, we run the risk of medicating unhealed pain within us, something we will discuss later in Chapter Twelve.

On the other hand, our destiny, where we are headed, is also based on a relationship with Jesus Christ and one day seeing Him face to face when our race is finished here on Earth.

Purpose is the culmination of all the acts or missions God has set out for us, which often include loving others, serving others, and sharing the Good News.

Through relationship with Christ, we are given both a destiny and purpose-filled life. In this relationship, God illuminates our spiritual gifting and empowers us to have a passion with purpose that makes an impact. We will discuss this more in Part Three.

As we proceed through this book, and in life for that matter, may we remember our jobs and tasks of the day are not what give us destiny.

Instead, our relationship with God gives us destiny, and through our relationship with Him, God orchestrates divine appointments for us to build purposeful lives.

To live like this requires humility and dedication, but as we begin to put less value on what our culture defines as purpose and more value on what God defines as purpose, we will not only have a greater impact, but we will experience a far more fulfilling life.

CHAPTER 10

THE PASSION OF SALVATION

———

Now it is God who makes both us and you stand
firm in Christ. He anointed us, set his seal of
ownership on us, and put his Spirit in our hearts
as a deposit, guaranteeing what is to come.

- 2 CORINTHIANS 1:21–22

Growing up attending Catholic school from kindergarten through high school, my faith was always incredibly important to me. I vividly remember wanting to be a priest when I was five, and most of my academic memories stem more from religion class than any other subject.

I grew up always hearing that "Jesus Saves," but I never took the time to understand what that actually meant and why it's important.

As discovered in the previous chapter, our salvation is the product of believing in Jesus Christ as the Messiah and Son of God who walked the Earth, was crucified, and resurrected.

The goal of this chapter is to dive deeper into why Jesus had to suffer the way He did for our salvation and discuss what this means not only for when we reach the end of our race as Believers, but also while we are running the race now and the impact this has on passion.

THE FALL

In the chapter War, Wrestling, & Passion, we talked about the war in heaven and how sin entered the world through the devil's temptation of Adam and Eve.

When Adam and Eve fell into temptation, the result was catastrophic.

Before the fall, Adam and Eve were in perfect harmony and relationship with God. They experienced fully what it was like to live a Spirit-led life as opposed to living a Soul-led life, driven by false emotions. They experienced a passion inspired by God's love as opposed to a passion expired by the enemy.

They rested in the peace of God and had a clear direction for their life where there was no pain, no stress, and no sadness. It was the closest thing to heaven on Earth, as the cliché goes.

By engaging in sin, Adam and Eve severed the union they had with God. The result was the elimination of eternal life and a soul fully engulfed by the temporal, carnal world without any oversight of the Spirit within them to guide them into everlasting life and stillness.

Their intuition, conscience, and communion with God was severed and, thus, they were left to build up their passion with the things of this world as opposed to the things of the Spirit.

THE FALLEN NATURE OF MAN

We have inherited the brokenness and fallen nature of Adam and Eve. Before faith in Jesus, our spirits are separated from God, and we are caught chasing our tails here on Earth directionless, as we are driven by our emotions and feelings, rather than an intellect and conscience that bears witness to the Holy Spirit.

Our souls are compromised, and we are prone to relentless assaults by the enemy to follow his way. In other words, our passion is critically compromised, and we have no ability to live a life with a passion fueled by God and His Spirit—a Spirit that inspires, encourages, and empowers us.

Just as our bodies are dead before the Lord and will experience mortality, our souls and spirit are dead before the Lord too before faith in Jesus. In essence, we are completely separated from God.

MANKIND'S RECONCILING TO RELATIONSHIP WITH GOD

The wage of sin and separation from God is death, as pointed out in Romans 6:23, but God had a plan to redeem humanity and His relationship with us. Better yet, he respects the free will He created us with and leaves it up to us, should we desire to know Him.

The only way to redeem our faith and allegiance to God is through confession of faith in Jesus Christ as the Messiah.

I am the way and the truth and the life. No one
comes to the Father except through me.

- JOHN 14:6 (NIV)

What Jesus is saying here is that through faith alone in Him, our relationship with God can be restored. But going along with the well-known saying, "Jesus Saves," we may be inclined to further ask why or how faith in Christ leads to eternal life and salvation.

The answer is rather simple but not all too often articulated, as it should be.

Our Creator is a just God, and by sending His one and only Son to take our place and pay the penalty of our sins, God fully applies the triune application of justice, mercy, and grace.

Let's break each of these down:

- Justice is when we get what we deserve.

- Mercy is when we don't get what we deserve.

- Grace is when we get what we don't deserve.

Through Christ's incarnation, crucifixion, and resurrection, our creator sacrificed His one and only Son, extending us grace, and paying the penalties we deserve for our fallen nature. Through this act of love lies a path to redemption, a path to reconciliation, and a path to divine relationship with our precious Creator, the Great Architect who fearfully and wonderfully made us and the path that lies before us.

Jesus paid it all, and He paid the price for you and me. Jesus stepping in and taking on the weight of our sins is coined by many theologians as penal substitution.

So when we say "Jesus Saves," we are saying Jesus was born, walked the Earth, served His Father in ministry, and then physically stepped in to take the place of the punishment we deserved for our fallen nature and sinful selves.

Jesus died for us not because we deserved it, but because God is just, merciful, and full of grace.

Remember, it wasn't God who severed our relationship. It was mankind who severed our relationship with God. Therefore, in order to reconcile our relationship with God, a penalty must be paid.

God desires to have a relationship with you and me. Again, not for His good, but for our good. God knows He cannot force us into a relationship with Him, but giving us the freedom to choose if we want to enter into a reconciled relationship with Him is the epitome of liberty, free will, and love.

And the path God took to provide us with this opportunity and by sacrificing Jesus is unconditional love.

All we need to do is have faith and believe in who Jesus says He is: the Messiah, our Lord, Our Savior, Emmanuel.

SALVATION NOW

As believers, it may be easy to fixate on eternal life, so much so that we forget we have salvation here and now while running our race. This is perhaps another key principle I want to discuss in this book.

When we discussed the Full Armor of God verse, one of the key elements of the armor was the helmet of salvation (Ephesians 6:17). Take notice how the helmet is used to represent salvation.

Salvation is not only pertinent to sharing eternal life with God, but salvation is also relevant now, as at the moment of faith in Christ, we experience an infilling of the Holy Spirit, where He comes to indwell within us and bear witness to our spirit.

Our spirit is no longer separated from God but is now in communion with God, and we experience a sanctified intuition, conscience, and communion.

Our souls are still in their fallen nature, but by the sanctification of Spirit, our soul can now choose life as opposed to choosing death, e.g., the path of culture and the world.

This is why I love the metaphor Paul the Apostle uses in Ephesians 6:17, describing salvation as a helmet. A helmet protects the head by covering it. It absorbs the impact of assaults. It protects from scraps and scrapes. It protects the most important organ of the physical body, the brain.

Now let's look at this spiritually. The soul is spiritually protected and guarded by the Spirit. Before having a sanctified spirit, we are led to fuel our soul and passion from the outside in with adverse effects. With a sanctified spirit, we are now able to choose how we will fuel our soul and passion.

The optimal path is to lead our souls into the care, protection, and provision of the Spirit.

Those who live according to the flesh have their minds set on what the flesh desires; but those who live in accordance with the Spirit have their minds set on what the Spirit desires. The mind governed by the flesh is death, but the mind governed by the Spirit is life and peace.

- ROMANS 8:5–6

The spirit protects the soul by covering it. It redirects the temptations of the enemy. It pours love into a wounded soul. It protects the most precious organ of our spiritual being.

When we come to understand our passion isn't a hobby, but rather something unique and personal to us, deep within us that is reactive to the internal and external worlds, which the ability to be our source of fuel to live out God's calling on our lives, there is just one source of fuel for our passion that can protect it from ever burning out: the sanctified Spirit.

It is through our Spirit and communion with God that our souls can experience the true love, goodness, and provision the Spirit has to offer.

God empowers us to live out our calling through a sanctified spirit, because when we are tempted to be led and driven by false emotions that may be compromised due to pain and traumas, God offers us an alternative source to fill the needs our passion requires to continue on our path forward.

Jesus was able to endure His suffering and the walk to Calvary not because of physical strength. Not because of will power. Not even because He is God.

Jesus was able to endure His suffering because He carried out His calling with a passion fueled by a sanctified Spirit. Jesus's passion was inspired by the Spirit. Jesus's passion was encouraged by the Spirit. Jesus's passion was empowered by the Spirit.

Jesus walked out His calling by walking in the Spirit, as opposed to walking in the flesh, which is solely motivated by what feels good.

We need to carry out our callings in life with a passion that will never burn out, even in times of adversity, pain, and suffering. By believing in Jesus, our passion becomes ignited and empowered by a sanctified spirit.

With a passion fueled by the Holy Spirit, one's passion will never burn out or be extinguished.

So I say, walk by the Spirit, and you will not gratify the
desires of the flesh. For the flesh desires what is contrary
to the Spirit, and the Spirit what is contrary to the flesh.
They are in conflict with each other, so that you are
not to do whatever you want. But if you are led by the
Spirit, you are not under the law. The acts of the flesh are
obvious: sexual immorality, impurity and debauchery;
idolatry and witchcraft; hatred, discord, jealousy, fits
of rage, selfish ambition, dissensions, factions and envy;
drunkenness, orgies, and the like. I warn you, as I did
before, that those who live like this will not inherit the
kingdom of God. But the fruit of the Spirit is love, joy,
peace, forbearance, kindness, goodness, faithfulness,
gentleness and self-control. Against such things there is
no law. Those who belong to Christ Jesus have crucified
the flesh with its passions and desires. Since we live by
the Spirit, let us keep in step with the Spirit. Let us not
become conceited, provoking and envying each other.

- GALATIANS 5:16–25

CHAPTER 11

KNOWING YOUR IDENTITY

———

Remain in me, as I also remain in you. No branch
can bear fruit by itself; it must remain in the vine.
Neither can you bear fruit unless you remain in me.

- JOHN 15:4

Before being the title for this book, Passion With Purpose was a student organization I started at Penn State with several other good friends. It was launched in 2015, but the ideas for it came as early as my freshman year in 2012.

Only a few weeks into my college experience, I couldn't help but notice the college culture engulfed by peer pressure and the immense challenges of authenticity faced by some of my closest friends and peers in my classes.

I noticed one of the biggest barriers for one building and living out their passion was the challenge of truly being authentic and living out their true identity.

For this reason, the motto for the club became Semper Authentica, the Latin translation for Always Authentic. Just as the War on Passion wages each day, so too does the battle to be truly authentic and live out our identity.

Just think about the family barbeques or networking events you go to. What's the first thing you say after you introduce your name? You typically say what you do. Interestingly enough, you do not introduce the action that you do. Instead, you apply an identity to it. I am an Engineer. I am a teacher. I am a police officer.

When God appeared to Moses in the burning bush and Moses asked what God's name was, God replied, "I AM WHO I AM." God didn't even refer to what He did as God. He introduced Himself as He is and who He is. God's value wasn't and isn't found in what He has done or what He does. His value is found in who He is.

Similarly, our value is found in who we are, not what we do. I think that culture confuses identity and action. There needs to be a distinction. As such, what we do for a living or what we do outside of a job or career is simply not our identity; rather, it is the application of our identity.

When I went to neuroscientist Dr. Caroline Leaf's conference in 2018, one of her talks was on identity and something she said still sticks out to me to this day: "When you lose your identity, you lose your hope. . . Labels lock you into a box. . . You are not a box."

Is your hope found in what you do or is it found in who you are? As I write this now amid the COVID-19 pandemic and think of the countless lives impacted and those who have lost their jobs or careers, my heart aches for those who have put their identity in what they do as opposed to who they are.

It's so easy to get caught up defining our identity based on what we provide to others; but there is another distinction to be made. Our identity provides value to someone while our job or work provides a good or service for someone.

This societal viewpoint is almost like saying your worth is dependent upon what you can provide for me. This is not how the Great Architect intended life to be.

God didn't sacrifice His one and only son so that we can provide goods and services to Him. God sacrificed His one and only son so we can be in relationship with Him and experience the fullness of who we were created to be, not just what we were created to do.

This is not to say God's intention was for us to sit around, idly watching Netflix. God's intention included us to come to the revelation of our spiritual giftings and callings and apply them to have purpose and impact in light of the eternal.

There will come a time in this world when all things will burn away, but it is the imprints on one another's souls we have that will last forever, not the trophy case, the skyscrapers we build, or the cities we build.

What lasts forever is the passion we build within one another.

God's intention for identity was to be found in Him, serving as an unshakeable and eternal identity—an identity that was and is and ever will be, which stays the same even when the seasons change.

If we put all of our identity into what we do, what happens when what we've done is no longer what we do? If your identity is being an engineer, what happens when you retire? If your identity is being an engineer and you are also a parent, are these competing identities? What a struggle to deal with within the soul.

We should seek to be transformed by an eternal identity that flows into everything we do and impacts everything we do.

Such an identity is an identity in Christ.

Before discussing what having an identity in Christ means, I would like to elaborate more on this idea of an eternal identity that doesn't change despite the seasons of life.

Let's look at a skyscraper. When a building rises above the streets, yes, we may be led to define the building by how it looks—maybe by even the type of companies that are tenants in the building. Some buildings are even named after the tenants that anchor the building!

But will the tenants or beautiful glass facade empower a building to withstand an earthquake or the power of wind and time?

Of course not.

It is the foundation of the building that empowers a building to remain resilient and stand the test of time despite the changes it undergoes.

We should develop our identity in something or someone that is forever eternal, firm and secure, never moving, and never shaking. This is the foundation on which we should build our passion. With a secure identity, we will be empowered to build up our passion regardless of the circumstances around us.

Your identity is at the core of who you are, just like the foundation and concrete center of a building is its core.

When companies move in and out of buildings as tenants, the floor plan is demoed, modified, and updated, but there is one building component that never changes during a tenant renovation. That is the core of the building: its identity.

When we put our identity in things like our jobs or in our relationships—things that change like the seasons—it's like putting our identity into a building's floor plan for a temporary tenant taking space in a skyscraper.

What happens when it goes away? Do you lose your identity, too? Do you lose who you are or what you do?

It is when we have identity in who we are that even if and when what we do changes, our passion is fueled by an ever-eternal identity.

This is why it's so important to have an identity in Christ first and foremost.

Let Jesus ground you and support your passion.

IDENTITY DEFINED

Before diving deeper into what it means to have an identity in Christ, let's clearly define identity. Thus far, we have confronted culture's definition of identity by redefining identity as who we are rather than what we do.

Simply put, what we do is the application of our identity, or as I like to say, putting passion into action.

A common thought is that our passion is our identity, but we must not include hobbies and external activities in this assessment.

As mentioned earlier in this book, passion is the thought, feeling, and choice experienced while doing the action. Thus, we build passion with our thoughts, feelings, and choices. With this in mind, we can now relate and define identity as one's passion.

In Dr. Caroline Leaf's book, The Perfect You: A Blueprint for Identity, she expounds upon this thought more clearly, proclaiming, "Your identity flows out of how you think, speak, and act."[73] All three of these actions flow forth from our

---

73 Caroline Leaf, *The Perfect You: A Blueprint for Identity* (Grand Rapids: Baker Publishing Group, 2017), 17.

soul and our passion. They flow from our thoughts, feelings, and choices.

The beauty of all this is that God created each of us with unique souls and unique personalities. Despite God desiring to have a relationship with us in which our Spirit leads our soul, God never imposes or forces His will upon mankind, nor does He seek to suppress the soul.

God desires for us to come to the fullness of who we are by expressing our true authentic selves through our soul. The presence of His Spirit bearing witness to our Spirit is what gives our soul life and its animation.

IDENTITY IN CHRIST

An identity in Christ is thus God serving as the foundation for how we can and should think, feel, and choose—how we execute our passion. Instead of others or ourselves telling us who we are, we rest in believing we are who God says we are. We put our hope in His promises over the "promises" of modern culture and we let His spirit of truth shape who we are and who we seek to become.

When we have an identity in Christ, our passion is grounded from the inside out as opposed to being grounded from the outside in.

The cultural definition of identity makes it about what we do outside of who we are, while God's blueprint for identity is about who we are based not on what others say about us, but what God says about us.

Before I formed you in the womb I knew you,
and before you were born I consecrated you; I
appointed you a prophet to the nations.

- JEREMIAH 1:5 ESV

Therefore, if anyone is in Christ, he is a new creation.
The old has passed away; behold, the new has come.

- 2 CORINTHIANS 5:17 ESV

Why, even the hairs of your head are all numbered. Fear
not; you are of more value than many sparrows.

- LUKE 12:7 ESV

Fear not, for I am with you; be not dismayed, for I
am your God; I will strengthen you, I will help you, I
will uphold you with my righteous right hand.

- ISAIAH 41:10 ESV

For God gave us a spirit not of fear but of
power and love and self-control.

- 2 TIMOTHY 1:7

Our worth and value is inherent and has and always will be.
Pause for a moment and take a breath.

You are worthy and have identity because you exist.

Before God formed you in the womb, He knew you.

Furthermore, even regardless of what we do and in spite of the mistakes and wrongs we make in life, we still have inherent worth and value because God commands it so.

God demonstrates His own love for us in this:
While we were still sinners, Christ died for us.

- ROMANS 5:8

Even with the chance mankind would choose not to believe and enter into relationship with Him through Christ and the sacrifice of His one and only Son, God still willed for Christ's crucifixion because you are worthy.

How beautiful it is to have value, worth, and identity regardless of what we do but based solely in who we are and in who God made us to be.

This is the beauty, power, and resilience of having a passion rooted in Christ that is inspired by God the Father, encouraged by the Son, and empowered by the Holy Spirit.

This viewpoint of identity is anti-cultural to society's worldview and understandably so, given the convictions and differences that come with a biblical worldview.

There is an important relationship between worldview and how it shapes our identity. The late apologist Ravi Zacharias most often referred to worldview as the associated thoughts with origin, meaning, morality, and destiny.

Answers to the questions "Where do we come from?" "What is my significance?" "What is right or wrong?" and "What happens to us after this life?" all play a part in shaping how we think, feel, and choose. They all play a part in how we interact with those around us and apply our passion.

BARRIERS TO IDENTITY & AUTHENTICITY

In Chapter Eight, Pete Scazzero talks about the temptations we have towards a false self or towards false identities. These false identities are rooted in emotional woundedness and pain—something we will discuss in the next chapter.

Scazzero categorized these false identities into three groups: Performance based (I am What I Do), Possession (I am What I Have), and Popularity (I Am What Others Think).[74]

Notice again how all of these have to do with our identity being defined from the outside in based on what others think and based on what we do.

These three false identities are also very similar to the three temptations of sin as noted in the scriptures.

For everything in the world—the lust of the flesh,
the lust of the eyes, and the pride of life—comes
not from the Father but from the world.

- 1 JOHN 2:16

---

74   Scazzero, *Emotionally Healthy Spirituality: It's Impossible to be Spiritually Mature While Remaining Emotionally Immature, Updated Edition*, 49–52.

A performance-based identity is rooted in the lust of the flesh. a possession-based identity is rooted in the lust of the eyes. A popularity-based identity is rooted in the pride of life.

These forms of identity stem from a secular humanist worldview definition of identity. Finite and flimsy, a passion rooted in an identity that lives off one's actions and the opinions of others will never withstand the adversity of life as does a passion rooted and grounded in having an identity in Christ.

God has shaped and crafted us internally—with a unique personality, thoughts, dreams, temperament, feelings, talents, gifts, and desires. He has planted "true seeds of self" inside of us. They make up the authentic "us." We are so deeply loved. We are a treasure.

- PETE SCAZZERO[75]

Even though we often place God as one thing among many other things, He never considers us as one thing among many other things. We are fearfully and wonderfully made with inherent worth and value.[76]

It is an identity in Christ that empowers us to transform one another's life while an identity in the world solely empowers us to provide a good or service to someone and not necessarily transform them.

---

75   Ibid., 50.

76   *Jon Leonetti*, "Building our Lives on God," April 18, 2014, video, 5:06.

Let us utilize our identity in Christ to ignite passion within one another as opposed to expiring the passion in one another. This will be a major theme of Part Three in this book.

CHAPTER 12

PASSION, PURPOSE, & THE INFECTED SOUL

———

Watch over your heart with all diligence,
for from it flow the springs of life.

- PROVERBS 4:23, AMP

Despite some of the adversity I faced, I did live a fortunate childhood. Growing up in a residential neighborhood in Staten Island, NY, all of my best friends lived within walking distance. One of my dearest friends, Victor, lived only two doors down from me. As kids, it was a race each morning to see who would knock on one another's door first to start off the summer days of fun.

From playing wiffle ball in the driveway and debating over what counted as a strike, to racing our bikes as fast as possible down the street, it was a textbook suburban childhood experience, something I'll always cherish to this day.

We were daring as kids, and like most kids growing up in the neighborhood, we all had our "battle scars." Let me clarify—not from one another, but from the pavement. Whether it was wrecking a bike or sliding on concrete and pavement to score a run, we definitely got into it with the pavement.

One time I was playing basketball with my friends and I took a tumble. I was pretty well-known for rolling around on the basketball courts, but that's a story for another day. My knee scraped against the pavement. As I grabbed my knee in agony, my friends picked me up as they always did. I looked down and found blood dripping down my knee, to no surprise. As I wiped some blood away with my dirty hands, I noticed pebbles and particles from the pavement embedded and interwoven with my scraped-up skin.

At this point, I realized I couldn't just wipe away the blood and keep playing, so I told my friends I would be back and limped on down back to my house to go see my mom. She had all the stuff for cuts and scrapes like these.

Before bandaging up the wound, my mom broke out the hydrogen peroxide. Oh, I hated hydrogen peroxide. I can see the image of that dark brown container that has been scarred into memory. As my mom chased me down with the hydrogen peroxide in her hand, eventually catching up and holding me down, she applied the peroxide. I knew the importance of the peroxide: to prevent infection. I realize today that we don't always enjoy the remedies we deeply need that lead to healing.

How often do we focus on physical health and physical healing and neglect the areas of mental and emotional healing? Even when we may bring up emotional healing after something like a breakup, we hear the cliché phrase, "Time heals all wounds." But would the scrape on my knee heal without the ointment my mom applied to prevent infection? Maybe it could have healed on its own, but it very well could have become infected without ointment.

Though the worlds of the physical and spiritual appear to be different, they are indeed similar. Just as a physical wound needs ointment in addition to time to heal, so too does the human soul! Throughout our lifetime, we will experience emotional traumas acting as wounds to the human soul. If left untreated or treated only by time, our souls risk becoming infected. The consequences of an infected soul are grave.

An infected soul leads to an infected passion. Rather than igniting and inspiring passion within others, an infected passion risks extinguishing and expiring the passion within others.

FROM SOUL WOUND TO SOUL INFECTION
Throughout most of my adolescence and throughout college, I suffered from severe anxiety and in particular obsessive-compulsive disorder. In college my anxiety manifested into depression as mentioned earlier in this book. I sought out therapy when I was nineteen. I knew there were things going on within me and I wanted to confront them once and for all. Deep down I knew the experiences I had growing up had a tremendous impact on me, and I knew there were voids within my heart. I just didn't know how to fill them. Aside from meeting with my therapist weekly, I met with a

priest on campus and asked him how I could fill the voids in my heart with God's love, but after that discussion I was still left searching.

I went to therapy consistently throughout college, but despite going for several years straight, I didn't experience any breakthroughs and my depression unfortunately changed into despair during my last year of college.

With nowhere left to turn, I made a phone call I will never forget. Standing outside of Gate A outside of Beaver Stadium while participating in PSU's infamous Nittanyville leading up to the big 2016 White Out Game against Ohio State, I called Christian psychologist Dominic Herbst.

I retreated away from the excitement of Nittanyville, ventured across the street outside of the baseball stadium, and paced back and forth as I called someone I knew nothing about, other than that the discipleship program he led had a profound impact on my dad's journey to restoration and healing.

On that phone call I poured my heart out to Dominic. His faith met my despair, and I could hear the confidence in his voice that I was about to embark on an incredible journey to healing I would have never thought possible.

Dominic's practice was just nearly a little over an hour from State College, PSU's campus. I started meeting with him on a weekly to biweekly basis during my final semester of college. Together we worked through what he calls "a journey through calvary" in his Restoring Relationships program, a resource recommended later in this book.

There were so many breakthroughs uncovered in this walk with Dominic, but one of the biggest was the power of an infected soul and how it can hold its captives in bondage.

When we experience an emotional wound in our lives, we experience the resulting feelings of the wounding initially, but with time, we eventually have control over how we respond. If we withhold acceptance or forgiveness, for example, our process of response can go from being on the pathway to healing to the pathway to infection.

In Dominic's Restoring Relationships Leadership Manual, he discusses two common responses to emotional trauma: anger and wrath. He references Ephesians 4:26 (KJV), which says, "Be ye angry, and sin not: let not the sun go down upon your wrath." Dominic notes that anger can "transform into rage which grows like a cancer within us and 'infect' our emotions."[77]

Later, Dominic teaches that anger comes from the Greek word "orge," which is an emotion we can control, while wrath comes from the Greek word "thumos," which describes "uncontrolled and unrestrained behavior that we are not able to control."[78]

When we are initially dealt an emotional wound, a healthy and normal response would be hurt and anger, but if we proceed forward without accepting the pain of our wounding and without walking through the reconciliation process, the original emotional wound can lead to a soul infection.

---

77   Dominic P. Herbst, *Restoring Relationships Resource Manual: "A Ministry of Reconciliation"* (Ashburn: Sonrise House Company, 2005), 39.

78   Ibid.

The risk with a soul infection is that it is catalyzed by wrath, namely the "thumos" wrath, which we are unable to control. This wrath roots itself within our emotions and overrides the faculties of our intellect and will.

We are then left with emotions influenced by past traumas driving and directing our intellect, thereby influencing our thoughts, words, and actions.

Soul infections are like gaping holes within our soul. The uncleansed pain within us drives us to seek out and search for any and all remedies around us. These manifestations vary from person to person, but some may include illicit relationships and substance abuse, perversion, impulsive behaviors, tendencies toward addiction, and more. Sometimes the remedies we chase after aren't so obvious, like a drug or alcohol addiction, and can appear innocent like a fixated focus on success or a tendency toward people-pleasing.

THE CANCER OF AN INFECTED SOUL

Another risk of the soul infection is that it can act like a cancer. Not only will the undealt-with pain and trauma in our lives contaminate our thoughts and choices, leading to unwanted behaviors and negative habits, but it can also impact the lives of others around us, especially those closest to us.

I vividly remember growing up in high school, thinking I didn't have any insecurities specific to relationships with others. It wasn't until my chapter of college that I realized how truly insecure I was in romantic relationships. I struggled with trust issues and jealousy, and the obsessive-compulsive disorder I had wrestled with for most of my adolescent years seemed to manifest itself whenever I was in a serious romantic relationship.

The fear and insecurity within me that was filled with trust issues made me depressed, and worse, it impacted my relationships. In fact, at times it felt like I had a monster inside of me. I knew my thoughts and fears were irrational, but I couldn't make them stop. I had no control. At full force, it felt as if my fear owned me. This fear filling my soul would then spill over into the soul of the person I was dating. It was a recipe that made for an unpleasant relationship.

I knew the insecurities I was dealing with were unhealthy and rather toxic. So, when I realized how the pain inside of me impacted others I deeply cared about, I began a journey through counseling at nineteen, as mentioned earlier.

I also knew deep down the issues I was dealing with as they related to dating had something to do with my parents' divorce and separation, but I just didn't know how to work through it.

I think therapy can do a great job of awakening someone to a pain point experienced in the past that is causing present adverse circumstances; but what's just as important, if not more important, is what we do with this awakened truth.

I knew the traumas I experienced from childhood were at play, but I still couldn't shake the struggles within me until I started working with Dominic. Through his program Restoring Relationships, he navigated me through the journey of going through my heart and namely the good and challenging experiences that left their mark on my soul.

Leading up to this moment, the soul infection within me had complete control over my emotions and behaviors when it came to romantic relationships. I entered into what Dominic calls a "pain for pain exchange" where if one doesn't know one's pain, they'll make another feel their pain.[79] My infected soul was no longer internal to me, but it became a cancer, infecting others around me.

All of this is so important to consider when we are striving to build a life of fulfillment, destiny, and impact because a lot of our fulfillment comes from deep and personal relationships. If we are unhealthy within, our relationships risk being unhealthy as well and will not reach the fullness of what they can become.

THE IMPACT OF AN INFECTED SOUL ON PASSION

When we are dealing with an infected soul, we can mistake our passions for what might actually be forms of self-medication, as a great remedy for pain is pleasure. Passion can so easily be misled because we can follow and do good things we are passionate about, but it is easy for these "passions" to become an idol for us.

Our passions and activities could stimulate such an arousal within one's soul that no matter how deep-rooted and seated the pain we may have within us, it is easy for that pain to

---

79 *Restoring Relationships*, "Marriage in Crisis," July 3, 2018, video, 2:35.

be masked by doing the things that make our thoughts and emotions feel good.

One can spend their entire life medicating the pains and traumas of their childhood, missing their purpose and fulfilling what they have been specifically called to do.

The good news, however, is that the Great Architect has designed and fulfilled the plans for us to reconcile with our past and reconcile ourselves back into relationship with Him, so we can truly build a life of fulfillment, destiny, and impact.

The design plans in question are that of Forgiveness and in the next chapter we will discuss the power reconciliation has to restore one's passion so it can be ignited, fueled, and sustained in the way God intended it to be.

CHAPTER 13

FORGIVENESS, RECONCILIATION, & PASSION

For if you forgive others their trespasses, your heavenly Father will also forgive you.

- MATTHEW 6:14, NMB

Only one path to healing an infected soul truly exists: the process of reconciliation in and through Jesus.

While Jesus was being readied for His crucifixion, He spoke out, "Father, forgive them, for they do not know what they are doing" (Luke 23:34).

One of Jesus's final acts while walking the Earth, before both reconciling Himself to the Father and creating a path for the world to reconcile itself to God, was forgiving those making an offense against Him.

In essence, there is no reconciliation without the intention of one's heart to forgive volitionally. By Christ's demonstration of forgiveness just before His final breath, we can learn quite a bit about what it means to forgive and how it relates to restoring one's passion to be fueled and put to use by the Holy Spirit.

Despite being flogged, mocked, ridiculed, rejected, and eventually put to death, Jesus expressed forgiveness for those making the offense against him. He asked God to forgive them and make it known those committing the offense didn't know what they were doing.

Despite the level of offense He endured by His aggressors, He had compassion for them. Both fully divine and human, Jesus experienced an offense.

An offense is like a knife that pierces the soul, leaving an emotional wound, and if left untreated, leads to an infection that can lead to certain manifestations—all of which we discussed in the previous chapter.

The Bible is clear. "It is impossible that no offenses should come" (Luke 17:1 NKJV). Offenses do not discriminate, and we are all prone to them. It's not a matter of if we will be offended, but rather how we will respond when offended.

One response leads to soul destitution while the other response leads to soul restoration.

As it relates to passion, one response leads to a soulish passion while the other leads to a soulical passion.

In his book, The Bait of Satan, John Bevere states the heart's true condition is naturally afflicted with pride. He notes that pride masks the impact of offense, leading one to repress an offense instead of confronting it.[80]

A repression of an offense leads to soul infection while confronting an offense is one of the first steps in healing from an offense.

Bevere notes, "Pride causes you to view yourself as a victim. . . Because you believe you are innocent and falsely accused, you hold back forgiveness. Though your true heart condition is hidden from you, it is not hidden from God. Just because you were mistreated, you do not have permission to hold on to an offense."[81] It is the response of holding on to an offense and repressing it that is the opposite path to reconciliation.

Such a response leads to a soul afflicted with wounding and pain, thus risking the chance to influence one's passions negatively.

This is why Bevere refers to offenses as a trap by the enemy: "Offense is a tool of the devil to bring people into captivity."[82]

Using pride and soul blinding to his advantage, the enemy deceives one into not forgiving an offender. Such a temptation is the sin of unforgiveness.

---

80 John Bevere, *The Bait of Satan* (Lake Mary: Charisma House, 2014), 7.

81 Ibid.

82 Ibid., 6.

THE SIN OF UNFORGIVENESS

The sin of unforgiveness is clearly spelled out in the Bible. This chapter kicked off with Matthew 6:14: "For if you forgive other people when they sin against you, your heavenly Father will also forgive you." The very next verse reads, "But if you do not forgive others their sins, your Father will not forgive your sins."

In the parable of the Unmerciful Servant in Matthew 18:21-35, a servant who debts are forgiven by his master later goes out and refuses to forgive the debts of another fellow servant. The result was catastrophic for the servant who was not willing to forgive his fellow servant.

As a consequence of his unforgiveness, the master handed him over to the jailers to be tortured. At the end of the parable, Jesus notes, "This is how my Heavenly Father will treat each of you unless you forgive your brother or sister from your heart" (Matthew 18:35).

There are several things to exegete from this parable and specifically the words of Jesus. First, notice how the master handed over the unmerciful servant to the jailers to be tortured. The master didn't torture the servant. The jailers did.

Applying this logic to us, when we sin against God, we in essence say no to God and yes to the enemy. By our sin, the enemy has liberty to attack us and wage war on us. We discussed such attacks at length in Chapter Six. Therefore, when we sin by withholding forgiveness, we not only offend God, but we welcome the enemy to come in and wage war on our soul, bring us into his captivity, and thus suffocate the fire of our passion.

Next, Jesus explicitly says we must forgive from the "heart." The original Greek word used here is kardia, which is literally defined as heart, but intentionally used to reference the inner self and specifically the will and volition of oneself.[83]

Forgiveness is an act of the will. It is intentional and especially spiritual. One can simply forgive with words, but if it is not grounded in true volition, it is not truly forgiveness.

This is why the enemy wages war on the soul and works to keep us blind within so we cannot internally see where we are wounded and where forgiveness is due.

Until we identify the offense, confront it, and forgive it from within, our passion risks being suffocated by the enemy and imprisoned by his ploys.

"Your fellowship with God flows freely when you're willing to forgive, but it gets blocked by unforgiveness. Forgiveness also keeps Satan from getting an advantage over us."

- JOYCE MEYER[84]

Anyone you forgive, I also forgive. And what I have forgiven—if there was anything to forgive—I have forgiven

---

83 Bible Hub, s.v. "2588. kardia," accessed February 12, 2021.

84 Joyce Meyer, "The Poison of Unforgiveness," *Joyce Meyer Ministries* (blog), accessed February 12, 2021.

in the sight of Christ for your sake, in order that Satan
might not outwit us. For we are not unaware of his schemes.

- 2 CORINTHIANS 2:10-11

Be angry but do not sin; do not let the sun set on
your anger, and do not leave room for the devil.

- EPHESIANS 4:26-27, NRSV

And they may come to their senses and escape from the
snare of the devil, after being captured by him to do his will."

- 2 TIMOTHY 2:26, ESV

A PASSION SUFFOCATED BY BONDAGE

An offense on the soul wounds the soul, but a trapped offense is what leads to a soul infection that compromises emotions, overriding the intellect and individual of a person.

At this point, the passion of one seeks to fuel itself by forms of self-medication and things of this world as opposed to fueling itself from the things of the Spirit.

When we fuel our passion with worldly desires in hopes of healing it, it is like filling a vase that has holes in it with water. It consumes but is never fulfilled or replenished. In essence, our passion becomes suffocated with the self and becomes more soulish.

The issue with a soulish passion is that it is separated from God and led by self. It is neither led by God nor sustained by

God. We will discuss this more in Part Three, but a soulish passion contains the risk of burning yourself out, or worse, negatively affecting others around you. Our passion can neither breathe itself nor can it truly ignite passion in others around us.

The enemy loves to keep us trapped in unforgiveness. Rather than God utilizing and sustaining our passion for His calling on our lives, the enemy can keep us in a state of passivity, or worse, use our passion to his advantage.

Unforgiveness opens the door for the enemy to have a foothold and as we knowingly or unknowingly but willingly withhold forgiveness, the enemy's grasp manifests into a stronghold and thus becomes harder to break free from.

The Gift of Reconciliation

All this is from God, who reconciled us to himself through Christ and gave us the ministry of reconciliation: that God was reconciling the world to himself in Christ, not counting people's sins against them. And he has committed to us the message of reconciliation. We are therefore Christ's ambassadors, as though God were making his appeal through us. We implore you on Christ's behalf: Be reconciled to God. God made him who had no sin to be sin for us, so that in him we might become the righteousness of God.
- 2 CORINTHIANS 5:18–21

In spite of the insurmountable offenses we will experience in our life (Luke 17:1), we must rejoice and be grateful for the gift of reconciliation that is available to us and freely given to us by Jesus.

To be reconciled means to be brought back into relationship or right standing with someone. The required action for reconciliation is that of volitional forgiveness.

As pointed out earlier in this chapter, one of Jesus's final acts was that of forgiveness. Being God Himself, Jesus still affirmed the process of reconciling Himself to the Father by forgiving those that have made offenses against Him.

This is perhaps an important lesson we must practice daily in our lives. Whether one intentionally offends us or unintentionally offends us, our souls are wounded by natural law.

The enemy will seek to keep us blinded of the offense by not only using pride, but by also influencing which offender we fixate on.

When it comes to relationships and offense, it can become rather complicated, but let's look at the case of divorce and the impact it has on children. Divorce ruptures and severs the foundation of the nuclear family. No divorce is the same, but on some occasions, a child may be hurt by one parent over the other. The result is the child developing conflict with that parent. It might look like forgiveness is only needed for the child towards the one parent the child is frustrated with, but in truth, that child must go through the process of forgiving each parent to truly break free from the sin of unforgiveness.

The sad truth is that in any divorce, the child or children affected is emotionally wounded by both parents. Even if, for example, the father abandons the family and the mother did nothing wrong, a child may unconsciously seek the consoling of the mother and seek to use the mother's love to heal the wounds within him or herself only God can heal.

In responding this way, the child's soul experiences unmet expectations toward the mother and in this case, the enemy can blind the child's heart in realizing there is forgiveness needed toward the mother. The other grave sin here is the inability or willful decision for the child to not trust God with his or her pain.

The enemy does not play by any rules and where there is unforgiveness, even when it is not conscious, the enemy comes flying in and feeds off of the pain and sin within one's soul.

But by God's mercy and the gift of the Holy Spirit, which we will discuss more in Part Three, it is through prayer and reflection that the Holy Spirit can shed light on where forgiveness is due in our lives so we can regularly reconcile our relationships with others and thereby reconcile our relationship with God.

The fact of the matter is that reconciliation isn't a seasonal activity. It must be intentional within one's will and also be constant.

In fact, when the Apostle Peter asked Jesus, "Lord, how many times shall I forgive my brother or sister who sins against me? Up to seven times?" Jesus answered, "I tell you, not seven times, but seventy-seven times" (Matthew 18:21–22).

At the last supper, Jesus gave a new commandment to His disciples, and thus to all of us: "Love one another. As I have loved you, so you must love one another" (John 13:34). The Greek word used for love by Jesus here is agape.[85]

There are numerous words for love throughout the Bible, but agape is profound. Agape is a spiritual, volitional, enduring, and sacrificial love that cannot be fully experienced and expressed without a relationship to God.[86]

It is with agape, a true sacrificial love, that we can embody forgiving hearts and truly forgive those who have trespassed against us.

The Bible in and of itself is a story of reconciliation, which does not happen without forgiveness. By Christ's model of sacrificing Himself and volitionally forgiving before His death, we too must forgive so we are reconciled back into relationship with God.

Through a reconciled relationship with God, our passion can truly be reconciled back into the lordship of the Great Architect so we can live with a passion that is spiritually grounded and eternally fueled to never burn out, regardless of circumstances.

With our passion we execute God's callings on our life and truly love others. We must guard our hearts (Proverbs 4:23) and let God's love flow through us and into the lives around us. Our true destiny in life is consistent reconciliation with God and our true purpose is making this agape known, felt, and expressed within others around us.

---

85   Bible Hub, s.v. "25. agapaó," accessed February 12, 2021.

86   Dominic P. Herbst, *Restoring Relationships Resource Manual: "A Ministry of Reconciliation"* (Ashburn: Sonrise House Company, 2005), 50.

CHAPTER 14

DESTINY – THE PURPOSE OF YOUR PASSION

———

Then Jesus said to them all: "Whoever wants
to be my disciple must deny themselves and
take up their cross daily and follow me".

- LUKE 9:23

Perhaps the biggest difference between a dream and a calling is that we chase dreams while callings chase us.

In the parable of the Wandering Sheep, Jesus tells a story about a man with one hundred sheep. When one of them wanders away, the Shepherd leaves the ninety-nine sheep to pursue the sheep who wandered off.

Jesus teaches through this parable that God pursues us in the same way. God doesn't put value or worth on quantity like we do in our culture; God places value on who we are because of who He created us to be and because of where He called us to.

In fact, while we were still trapped in our sin, Christ still died for us, reconciling us back into relationship with God (Romans 5:8).

Each of us have inherent worth being made in the image of God; we have precious value because God has gifted and called each of us to fulfill a calling on our lives, not only because it can bring Him glory, but also because our calling can and will transform the lives of others around us.

Spiritual purpose is not simply providing a good or service to someone.

Spiritual purpose transforms the hearts of others around us.

But in order to have a true purpose and be able to discern our calling and fulfill it, we must have a destiny—this destiny is a reconciled relationship with God. When we place our trust and hope in Christ, we not only receive the destiny of seeing Him face to face when our race on Earth is finished, but we also receive that destiny now. The same Spirit that raised Jesus from the grave resides within us at the moment of confession that Jesus is Lord over our life, specifically our soul and our passion.

Our relationship with Jesus doesn't begin when we reach heaven. Our relationship with Jesus began before we were even formed in our mother's womb. By reconciling our relationship to God through Jesus, we are equipped to discern our calling from God and then are encouraged by Jesus in fulfilling it.

The use of the word encouragement here is intentional and significant. In Part Three, we will break this down more, but encouragement aids and serves human emotion.

The reality is, it's one endeavor to hear and understand our calling, but it's another challenge to truly live out our calling with a passion fueled by a relationship with God.

We will continue to face adversity in life and especially emotional offenses dealt to us by others. We must not mistake a life of fulfillment and destiny with one of having all we've ever wanted from a materialistic perspective. Do not forget that passion is an experience and comes from the word that literally means to suffer.

This is why Jesus tells us in the synoptic gospels we must deny ourselves and take up our crosses daily, and why it states in the book of Galatians to crucify our flesh with its passions and desires (Galatians 5:24).

While we continue to run this race on Earth, our flesh will always and persistently war against our spirit (Galatians 5:17). Between selfish desires and personal attempts at medicating soul infections, our passion risks being controlled by our soulish self and by the enemy.

But by God's divine plan, we have been given the gift of reconciliation and more specifically, given an opportunity to come into relationship with Jesus, who is the Great Physician.

While we will be tempted to self-medicate the trauma in our lives with sin, whether that be explicit or implicit sin, we must be persistent and trust that Jesus is our only true physician. Jesus heals the soul by first healing our emotions.

God may navigate us through challenging seasons in our lives, not to punish us, but to put us in a position to trust Him more so He can work in us in a way only He can do. One can only be healed and saved if they wish to be so. Jesus does not force His healing hand on us, but it is available to us.

When I began my career in the Pocono Mountains, isolated from family and friends, I was so bitter toward God. It was perhaps the complete opposite of what I thought I needed to heal from my last year of college, when I faced severe depression. It was only a matter of months into my career when my depression reached the darkest it had ever been.

But through that experience, God put me in a position where I had no one and nothing to trust for healing other than Him. As I quieted myself and let God wrap His healing hands around me, I began to experience Him. Continuing to grow in knowledge of Him comforted my intellect, emotion, and will.

It was not an easy experience by any means. Throughout my entire time in the Poconos, I felt as if I was a child being held down on the hospital bed by my Dad, as the doctor applied medication. To this day I envision myself in the Poconos as flailing around with rage, with Jesus holding me down so God the Father and the Holy Spirit could operate on my soul, healing it and truly restoring my passion.

When we build a life encouraged by the Great Physician, Jesus Christ, we live each day with the intent to grow in relationship with Jesus and most importantly earnestly seek to trust Him to be the soul keeper and caretaker of our souls. The question we must ask ourselves is: will we trust God with our pain?

This journey is not an easy one. The Apostle Paul describes himself as having a thorn in his flesh (2 Corinthians 12:7–10).

In spite of all the pain and thorns we experience daily in our lives, how do we truly live out and fulfill our calling from God?

As stated before, we live it out with a passion fueled by God, which is built upon the foundation of relationship with God. The purpose of our passion is to be the fuel and mechanism by which we fulfill our calling, have purpose, and transform the lives of others around us.

Our passion, the fire within us, will continually and persistently undergo trials, temptations, and persecutions, but by continually renewing our mind and by constantly building our passion up with the tools and materials of inspiration, encouragement, and empowerment, we can fulfill our calling with a passion that doesn't burn out.

Such a journey is what I like to call the "art of passioneering," and the central figure of this discipline of "engineering" is the Holy Spirit. It's now time to move into Part Three of this book and put into action all we have learned in Parts One and Two; this way we can experience daily the purpose of our passion and build a life empowered by the Great Life Coach, the Holy Spirit.

PART THREE

IMPACT

BUILDING A LIFE EMPOWERED
BY THE GREAT LIFE COACH

Let us look out, being equipped by the Great
Life Coach, the Holy Spirit, and edify the
passion within ourselves and within others
around us.

CHAPTER 15

THE ART OF
PASSIONEERING

———

Therefore encourage one another and build
each other up, just as in fact you are doing.

- 1 THESSALONIANS 5:11

When I first began my journey at Penn State as an engineering major, I first entered to learn, but it wasn't long until I began to serve. With an innumerable number of opportunities to get involved in service activities and get involved with organizations making a difference both on campus and abroad, I quickly became more fixated on the opportunity I had to make a difference rather than simply earning a degree in architectural engineering.

In many classes (not all!), I often dozed off due to late nights and all-nighters, or I was tuned out of class and trying to get some work in for the organizations I was involved with. This definitely made life a little stressful, and I still reflect on the fond memories where my friends would take selfies with me sleeping in class or teach me how to design a lighting layout for a building, just minutes before an exam. Talk about adrenaline. Yikes!

I was so fortunate to have been a student leader working alongside so many incredible, dedicated, and driven students. I learned how to solve problems through math and science in engineering school, but through my extracurriculars I learned how to impact the hearts of those around me through love, compassion, and empathy.

I quickly added the words inspiration, encouragement, and empowerment to my tool kit when it came to leading others and making an impact.

During my college experience, the term Passioneering was born, but after experiencing a breakthrough in my faith journey during my final year, the term passioneering took on a more significant and deeper meaning.

In the Church, we often hear the words evangelism and discipleship. Unfortunately, we often separate these words when they should be brought together and applied in every teaching lesson, every sermon, and every conversation. Furthermore, we can get so fixated on evangelism and discipleship that we forget about the need of edification as believers.

🔥 **Evangelism** is leading one into faith.

🔥 **Discipleship** is learning and growing in the faith.

🔥 **Edification** is encouragement and building one another up.

Passioneering is edification in action through the applications of evangelism and discipleship. It is edifying others not simply within their soul, but by building their soul up. Passioneering is building up one another's relationship with God, ushering one's soul into the governance of the Spirit. Where the Spirit of the Lord is, there is freedom, liberty, and empowerment (2 Corinthians 3:17).

You see, just as there are roadblocks on the path of life and constraints on construction project sites, there are also roadblocks, constraints, and strongholds separating us from the direction of the Spirit and a deeper relationship with God. These roadblocks include sin, Satan, and self, which limit the ability for our passion to be cultivated, fostered, and empowered by the Holy Spirit.

The art of Passioneering is actively and intentionally removing these roadblocks. Passioneering is something we can do for ourselves, but it is most impactful when carried out within community when we can serve as passioneers for one another. When we remove the roadblocks and barriers to passion, we open up the pathways for the love and fruits of the Holy Spirit to guide, cultivate and fuel our passion. Such fruit includes: love, joy, peace, forbearance, kindness, goodness, faithfulness, gentleness, and self-control (Galatians 5:22–23).

With this in mind, let's discuss the roadblocks and barriers to passion.

SIN

Although I grew up in the church, my perspective of sin was that it made you a bad person and that you should simply do everything you could do without sinning. It was a very moralistic and legalistic perspective. But it isn't morals that first create the relationship between God and man. Morals don't start the relationship with God; instead, they sustain our relationship with God.

As we discussed in Part Two of this book, humble surrendering of oneself into relationship with Christ creates an intimate relationship with God. Through our choice, we enter into relationship with Christ, and through our actions we sustain and maintain that relationship with Christ. God has already done His part, but we must do ours. To be clear, it isn't God departing from us, but it is we who depart from Him and not remain in His love as coined in John 15:9.

Once we believe in Jesus, sin does not end our relationship with God or eliminate our salvation, but it does separate us from God. I like to think of sin and our relationship with God like cholesterol in arteries.

We are eternally connected with God. While here on Earth there is an artery connecting us to the presence, love, and joy of God; within this artery the blood of life flows from His Spirit, to our Spirit, and then to our soul, never ending and eternally flowing. But when we sin, we add cholesterol to this artery, and as our sin grows, the cholesterol in this eternal artery grows, eventually so much so that it separates our Spirit and Soul to the point that we cannot discern the love and voice of God. Sin does not make the presence of the Spirit go away, it just numbs us to His presence, leading us down the path of living a life dictated by our fleshly and carnal being.

One of the ways to Passioneer ourselves and others is by working to eliminate and minimize sin in our lives. We are fallen creatures and until the day we are united one with Christ in Heaven, we will always fall prey to temptation and unfortunately act on our sin.

But the goal to keep in mind here is to foster a desire deep within our souls to be close to God and close to His Spirit. Because our thoughts and feelings can be so easily swayed, it is through listening to our Spirit that we can keep our passion healthy and directed. We must hate sin and understand that not only does it hurt our relationship with God, but it also hurts us!

Yes, sin may feel pleasurable and materialistic and bring that momentary false sense of fulfillment, but it will never measure up to the joy that relationship with our Father brings. The other issue with sin is that it can keep us stuck or give us tunnel vision for the path we see for our lives.

Later in Part Three we will discuss more of the relationship of the Spirit and the Soul. WIthout the Spirit, our soul would be driven by our thoughts and feelings, which are easily tampered, influenced, and misled by our self, others, and especially the enemy.

GOOD VS. EVIL

Another roadblock between us and God is the war between Good and Evil. As discussed in Part One, this war has already been won by God in and through Christ and His crucifixion and resurrection; however, the prince of the Earth is the devil (2 Corinthians 4:4) and he still wages war on the human soul to keep us in bondage, out of the will of God, and especially with a passion under his control and influence.

It is through our relationship with God that one can discern his or her calling and then live it out with a passion fueled by the Holy Spirit. We must be aware and on guard of how the Enemy can and will utilize pleasure, temptation, and sin to not only separate us from God, but also do everything in his power to keep us from walking out God's purpose and destiny for our lives. We must realize we are an enemy of Satan and his army, and that they see us as a weapon and instrument of God to make a difference in this world and to lead other human beings to relationship with God and away from the bondage of the enemy.

THE SELF

We are also our own worst enemy oftentimes. Sin and self are so entangled sometimes, mostly because the selfish desires of the self are not only sins themselves, but can also lead to more sin and outward behaviors and acts of sin.

As discussed throughout this book, it should be our aim to be soulical believers as opposed to being soulish believers. In essence, being soulish is being selfish, meaning we live based on feeling rather than conviction.

Tim Tebow says, "Your emotions will never be consistent. Sometimes they'll be good, but sometimes they'll lead you astray. On the contrary, your convictions are rooted in your belief and principles and will lead you to your calling."[87]

---

87 Tim Tebow, "If You're Someone Who Always Listens to their Emotions, You Need to Stop," *Tim Tebow* (blog), accessed February 13, 2021.

It's important to be led by conviction because conviction occurs in the faculty of conscience within one's Spirit where our Spirit is led by the Lord.

As we discussed in Part Two, we must be hesitant about the amount of power and truth we give to our feelings as they can be so easily infected and influenced by unhealed pain and traumas in our lives. I am not saying to completely disregard your feelings and not listen to them. Instead, I am saying to test your feelings with your Spirit to see what is good and true (James 1:17).

Bringing our emotions into the presence of the Lord is a huge step in magnifying our passion. God wants us to cast aside the harmful emotions and utilize our healthy emotions to fulfill our callings and purpose. The Spirit of God can help us discern and distinguish the healthy emotions from the unhealthy emotions.

We must always remember we aren't machines. When we come to faith in Christ, we aren't supposed to completely turn off our soul, but work daily toward captaining our soul based on the Lord's leading rather than the leading of the self.

When we are able to go from soulish to soulical, we eliminate the selfish threats we may have within us that the enemy can use to keep us away from what God has called us to do.

A mentor of mine once said a good thing isn't always the God thing. We must always be self-aware and take internal inventory to know what is going on deep within ourselves.

We must ask ourselves if the things we think or do are under the direction of the self or under the direction and gentle leading of the Holy Spirit. With this question, we can discern whether the thoughts and actions we have and do are in fact the God things or the good things. Why settle for the good thing when the God thing is for us on our path? Even the enemy can use the good thing to distract us from the God thing.

THE ART OF PASSIONEERING

As engineers remove roadblocks and constraints and solve problems so builders can build, so too do you and I have an eternal call to remove the roadblocks of sin, Satan, and self so we can truly build a life of fulfillment, destiny, and impact in and through Jesus.

By passioneering, we are engineering the relationship between God and man. We are closing the gap between the Spirit and the Soul so when our passion burns, it burns with an energy that can never burn out no matter what adversity or temptation the enemy puts in our way to distract us or expire our passion.

Passioneering is important to build passion as it not only helps us remove these roadblocks on the path of a deeper and more defined relationship with God, but it also helps us build one another up through the tools of a Passioneer, which we will unpack in the chapter on the Passioneer's Blueprints.

Being a Passioneer is an important role we should all take on with pride. We are all instruments of love and joy. We cannot escape suffering and pain in this life. Jesus is the answer to all of our pain and struggles, but God uses each of us as satellites and vessels to carry his love and hope of salvation from one person to the next.

In all we do, let's be quick to inspire, encourage, and empower others around us with the hope of our relationship with God and with the hope we have in the Great Architect's Blueprints, the Word of God.

A necessary step; however, is taking the path forward in owning our struggles and passions through the power of the Holy Spirit.

It is when we own our passion that we can truly encourage one another and build each other up as we are called to do.

This is what it means to have impact.

CHAPTER 16

OWNING YOUR STRUGGLES

———

But he said to me, "My grace is sufficient for you, for my power is made perfect in weakness." Therefore I will boast all the more gladly about my weaknesses, so that Christ's power may rest on me.

- 2 CORINTHIANS 12:9

Have you ever wondered if it's possible to proceed through life without experiencing or enduring struggle? Is success and fulfillment a life absent from struggle or is it measured by the ability to endure and wrestle with struggle? Or maybe it has to do with how we own our struggle and our passion? We will address such questions throughout this chapter.

The world we live in today is overridden with the pursuit of identity. One common identity is that of one's identity being their struggle. But if our identity is found in our struggle, does our struggle own us or do we own our struggle?

What comes to mind is my struggle with mental health during college, and specifically during my final year of school and as I began my career.

I understand this is a delicate topic, and I am by no means a psychologist or psychiatrist, so please take note of this disclaimer. Issues regarding mental health are real, severe, and require intervention at the discretion of your doctor or primary care physician.

With this in mind though, I wish I could say solely seeking medical attention with the help of a psychiatrist and going on medication helped me break free from my depression and anxiety. If I am being honest, my personal experience of going down the path of medical diagnosis and medication actually did more harm than good.

You see, I thought if I could just get that clinical diagnosis and come under that identity as one with depression, I would then be able to truly heal.

But I was confronting the wrong issue. I was confronting the depression and not the areas of my life that lead to my depression in the first place. I had developed a victimhood mentality and put my identity in my struggles more than anything else.

My depression owned me.

But then I had a breakthrough in my faith journey. While rediscovering my relationship with Jesus, I realized that He isn't only the Messiah but also the Great Physician. Then things began to change. I started to have hope, and I began to start taking ownership over my life and my struggle with depression.

I began to change my identity from a mental health struggle identity to an identity grounded in Christ as I continued the journey of reconciling with my past experiences and learned about all the biblical figures who had endured struggle. Just to mention a few:

Elijah - "I have had enough Lord, he said. Take my life, I am not better than my ancestors." - 1 Kings 19:4

Jonah - "Now O Lord, take away my life, for it is better for me to die than to live." - Jonah 4:3

David - "My God, my God, why have you forsaken me? Why are you so far from saving me, so far from my cries of anguish?" - Psalm 22:1

Paul the Apostle - "And lest I should be exalted above measure by the abundance of the revelations, a thorn in the flesh was given to me, a messenger of Satan to buffet me, lest I be exalted above measure." - 2 Corinthians 12:7 (NKJV)

Many throughout the Bible have faced immense suffering and struggle, and we can all learn something from the Apostle Paul as he referred to his struggle as a thorn in his flesh.

OUR STRUGGLE IS NOT OUR IDENTITY

To this day, it is not clear what Paul's thorn was, but he intentionally did not name it or give it an identity. Paul's identity was not defined by what he was struggling with; it was defined by how he struggled with it—by taking His struggle before God.

TAKING OUR STRUGGLE TO THE LORD

When discussing his thorn, Paul pleaded for God to remove it three times, but God didn't remove it. Instead, His response was, "My grace is sufficient for you, for My strength is made perfect in weakness" (2 Corinthians 12:9 NKJV).

Paul's pursuit of the Lord in his struggle was persistent. Even though Paul didn't get the answer to his prayer that he desired, God made it clear the path forward was to completely and fully trust God with his struggle.

All we truly need is grace alone by faith alone to not only own our struggle, but also to not let our struggles get in the way of our calling and undermine our passion.

GOD'S STRENGTH MADE PERFECT IN WEAKNESS

As we let God into our struggles and let go as we "let God," we permit Him to perform the healing and empowering only He offers. How often do we get in the way of what God can provide us?

One of the most important steps in owning our struggle is surrendering it to God, but sometimes our own pride and knowledge can get in the way.

King Solomon, perhaps the wisest person to have ever lived, ended up battling despair and his own demise despite all he accomplished. "Yet when I surveyed all that my hands had done and what I had toiled to achieve, everything was meaningless, a chasing after the wind; nothing was gained under the sun" (Ecclesiastes 2:11).

In Ken Baugh's writing of The Big Idea, an Introduction to Warren W. Wiersbe's Be Skillful: God's Guidebook to Wise Living, Baugh attributes the demise of Solomon's struggle to three sins. Solomon did not trust in the protection of the Lord, the promise of the Lord, and the provision of the Lord.[88]

The action of trust is the expression of the human will and volition.

To trust is a decision and through trusting in God's protection, promises, and provision, we can truly let him into our deepest areas of need so He can engage in our struggles alongside us and within us.

When we surrender the struggles out of our control into His hands, we can truly own our struggle.

THE WILL & PASSION

Throughout Part One, the focal aspect of the soul we discussed was the human intellect. In Part Two, the faculty of the soul we explored was the human emotion.

---

88 Warren W. Wiersbe, *Be Skillful: God's Guidebook to Wise Living* (Colorado Springs: David C Cook, 2009), 7–10.

The faculty that will be the central figure of Part Three is the human will.

Serving as the decision-making organ of our being, it is our will that is at the conclusion of the Soul-Action-Sequence manifesting our outward behaviors and thus the passion we build up from within.

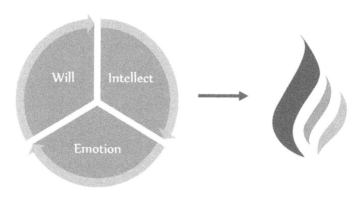

Figure 16.1: Soul-Action-Sequence by Steven F. Mezzacappa

The Soul-Action-Sequence is used to demonstrate the sequence of events that happen within our soul, impacting the fire and passion within us and leading to outward behaviors.

The will plays one of the most important roles in this sequence because it decides to be passive or active. Our thoughts and feelings can stir within, propelling us forward with action or inaction. It is our will that ultimately decides.

The theme of Free Will is all throughout Scripture and is at the core of Christian belief. As discussed previously, through our free will and decision to submit our lives to the kingship of Christ, we receive salvation, and most importantly, the gift of the Holy Spirit.

With this same free will, we decide whether or not to take ownership of the struggles we endure.

When I was just a little under a year into my career outside of college, my depression had hit a point lower than it had while I was in college. No longer on medication and only meeting with a counselor several times a month, I consciously made the decision to own the season I was in.

At this point, I was maturing in my faith, and deep down I knew God would restore the passion within me. I desired to and willed to trust in God's protection, promises, and provision over my life. It was not an easy season, but I believe deep down rejecting the identity of depression and instead placing my identity and faith in Christ put me on a path to true restoration and healing.

It was not an overnight experience. It was a gradual process, and it was the furthest thing from a clean path. Every day was a battle, but I learned to separate my struggle from who I was.

Struggle is not intended by God to be our identity. If it were, maybe Paul's thorn would have been specifically labeled.

Struggle is a fact of life. When we make our struggle our identity, it owns us. When our struggle owns us, it dominates our passion, the tool we use to endure our struggles so we can continue down the paths God has called us to.

*Struggling is not the identity. You must learn to
live while you struggle, such that anyone who sees
you can separate the struggle from your life.*

- UNKNOWN.[89]

When our identity is in Christ, we enable the Holy Spirit to be oxygen and fuel for the passion that burns within us. As long as our struggle owns us, we will always be at a disadvantage. A struggle that owns us not only risks extinguishing our passion, but it also impedes the opportunity to grow and be molded by these struggles.

When Jesus was in the Garden of Gethsemane on the Eve of His Crucifixion, he didn't try to avoid or evade the situation and imminent struggle. Jesus owned His struggle by confronting it head on and by taking it to the Lord and creating a pathway for the Holy Spirit to work through Him and sustain Him on His journey of purpose.

Owning our struggles so we are always in a position to fulfill our calling and to love those around us may seem like an impossible task. But it only seems that way when we seek to achieve this in our own strength and when the adversity we endure is beyond human explanation.

We must always remember God's strength is made perfect in our weakness, not because of our effort, but because of our

---

89   Davis Macron, "31 Inspirational Quotes About Life and Struggles," *The Right Messages*, October 1, 2018, accessed February 15, 2021.

choice to put our hope in God and trust in his protection, promise, and provision.

The more we surrender, the more God will grab onto and sustain us through our struggles. God accomplishes this through the power of the Holy Spirit that resides within us.

CHAPTER 17

THE HOLY SPIRIT & YOU

———

I will ask the Father, and he will give you another advocate to help you and be with you forever.

- JOHN 14:16

At the beginning of this book was the Latin phrase Veni Sancte Spiritus, which means "Come Holy Spirit." I first heard this phrase when I attended speaker, author, and radio host Jon Leonetti's "Surge for the Heart" retreat back in college.

It was the year prior to my final year of college and just so happened to be the semester before my dreams were met with unexpected disappointment and loss. Looking back, I shouldn't have been surprised though. Attending this retreat required me to drive to a Catholic church off campus several nights in a row right in the middle of the semester.

My soul and passion were seeking to be fed by God. I just wasn't conscious of it.

Have you ever paused to take self-inventory and ask yourself why you do the things you do? Are you searching something or someone out? Are you trying to be comforted? Are you seeking guidance or counsel? Are you seeking an advocate?

I know I was seeking all of the above as I sat in class one day in anguish battling my anxiety and depression. After a heart-wrenching journal entry, I scribbled the prayer Jon had taught us at the retreat: Come Holy Spirit. Be Kindle in Us. The Fire of Your Love.

I knew I was asking the Holy Spirit to give me strength in that moment, but I didn't realize then the Holy Spirit provides so much more than strength in our times of need. In fact, the Holy Spirit is our greatest source of fuel when it comes to empowering the passion and fire within us. Let me explain.

At the Last Supper, after Jesus had predicted His death, His betrayal, and Peter's denial, it got gloom and doom pretty quick. To comfort His disciples, Jesus did three distinct things to bring comfort to their souls aside from praying for them. He inspired them. He encouraged them. He empowered them.

HOW JESUS INSPIRES

Jesus inspired His disciples by instructing them with truth. He said, "Do not let your hearts be troubled. You believe in God; believe also in me. My Father's house has many rooms; if that were not so, would I have told you that I am going there to prepare a place for you? And if I go and prepare a place for you, I will come back and take you to be with me that you also may be where I am. You know the way to the place where I am going" (John 14:1–4).

Jesus spoke life into His disciples by reminding them of the gift of their salvation and guided them to fix their eyes on eternity rather than the temporary. Jesus guided them to lean on the solid rock of truth, rather than on the loose sand of humanistic perspective.

HOW JESUS ENCOURAGES
Jesus encouraged His disciples by affirming to them His authority and the authority He gave them.

When Thomas asked Jesus, "How can we know the way?" Jesus answered, "I am the way the truth and the life. No one comes to the Father except through me."

Philip unwittingly replied, "Lord, show us the Father and that will be enough for us."

Jesus answered Philip, "Anyone who has seen me has seen the Father. How can you say, 'Show us the Father'? Don't you believe that I am in the Father, and that the Father is in me? The words I say to you I do not speak on my own authority. Rather, it is the Father, living in me, who is doing his work. . . Very truly I tell you, whoever believes in me will do the works I have been doing, and they will do even greater things than these, because I am going to the Father. And I will do whatever you ask in my name, so that the Father may be glorified in the Son. You may ask me for anything in my name, and I will do it" (John14:5–14).

Jesus reaffirmed His identity as savior to his fearful disciples and gave them courage by communicating His authority and the authority His disciples would now receive when Jesus returned to the Father. The disciples should remain encouraged because they had the strength to do many things in the name of Christ.

HOW JESUS EMPOWERS

Finally, Jesus empowered His disciples by promising them the Holy Spirit. He said to them, "If you love me, keep my commands. And I will ask the Father, and he will give you another advocate to help you and be with you forever—the Spirit of truth. The world cannot accept him, because it neither sees him nor knows him. But you know him, for he lives with you and will be in you" (John 14:15–17).

Here, Jesus makes a reference to the Holy Spirit. The word for advocate Jesus uses to describe the Holy Spirit is the Greek word parakletos. This word is a compound word comprised of the two Greek words: para and kaleo.[90]

The word para means "besides" or "to come alongside," and the word kaleo means "to beckon or to call."[91] Bringing these two words together, the Holy Spirit serves as our advocate and helper by being alongside us and speaking to us gently.

---

90 Bevere, *The Holy Spirit: An Introduction*, 22.

91 *The Religion Teacher*, "The Meaning of Paraclete (Holy Spirit) in the Bible," June 11, 2019, video, 2:14; John Bevere, *The Holy Spirit: An Introduction* (Palmer Lake: Messenger International, 2013), 22.

John Bevere defines it best in his book The Holy Spirit: An Introduction: "The Holy Spirit is permanently called closely alongside each of us to provide coaching, direction, instruction, and counsel in our life Journey."[92]

DIGGING DEEPER INTO WHO THE HOLY SPIRIT IS

The Holy Spirit is specifically referenced ninety-six times in Scripture. The Spirit of the Lord is mentioned twenty-eight times, and the Spirit of God is mentioned twenty-six times. Throughout the rest of the Bible, the Holy Spirit is also referenced as the Eternal Spirit, Helper, Comforter, Holy One, The Lord, Spirit of Truth, Spirit of Christ, Spirit of Jesus Christ, Spirit of Counsel, Spirit of Knowledge, Spirit of might, Spirit of understanding, Spirit of wisdom, Spirit of the Lord, Spirit of your Father, Spirit of glory, Spirit of grace, Spirit of judgement, Spirit of burning, Spirit of life, Spirit of love, Spirit of power, Spirit of mind, Spirit of prophecy, Spirit of revelation, Spirit of holiness, and Spirit of the Holy God.[93]

When we come into relationship with Jesus Christ, the Holy Spirit comes and bears witness to our Spirit. This is the same Spirit that raised Christ from the dead (Romans 8:11). Remember parakletos means speaking alongside us. The indwelling of the Holy Spirit is how God guides, teaches, and comforts us. In essence, the Holy Spirit empowers us and is our life coach. The Holy Spirit is the Divine Life Coach. He is the ultimate and the Great Life Coach.

---

92 Ibid.

93 Bevere, The Holy Spirit: An Introduction, 18–19.

Our relationship with the Holy Spirit is intimate and precious and through His equipping and empowering we can continually fan into flames our spiritual gifts and ignite our passion.

When it comes to the word Empower, Google has two definitions: [94]

1. To give (someone) the authority or power to do something.

2. Make (someone) stronger and more confident, especially in controlling their life and claiming their rights.

The Holy Spirit does not force us to make decisions or pressure us like the enemy does. Instead, He gently guides us and leads with love, ushering in liberty and empowering us to exercise our free will to its full potential. The Holy Spirit is our counselor, helper, intercession, advocate, and strengthener.

HOW DOES THE HOLY SPIRIT EMPOWER?

As Jesus continued to comfort His disciples, He spoke to them also about the works of the Holy Spirit. "But when he, the Spirit of Truth, comes, he will guide you into all the truth. He will not speak on His own; he will speak only what he hears, and he will tell you what is yet to come. He will glorify me because it is from me that he will receive what he will make known to you. All that belongs to the Father is mine. That is why I said the Spirit will receive from me what He will make known to you" (John 16: 13-15).

---

94 "Empower," Google, accessed February 19, 2021.

When it comes to empowering someone, there are two items that must be evident: providing someone with the liberty and authority to make their own decision and also a degree of equipping.

As mentioned, the Holy Spirit does not force us to make decisions in our will, but instead, He makes known to us what the Father makes known to Him. This is how God communicates to us. We must not get distracted by what is fancied in the movies. If we lived our lives solely looking to hear God in a burning bush like He appeared to Moses, we may be gravely disappointed.

This is not to say God won't use awe, wonders, and miracles to communicate to us. He sure can. But we must not miss out on how God communicates to us, because it is more often than we realize.

The Father makes known to the Spirit what must be known, and then the Holy Spirit communicates with our personal spirit, or inner man, as mentioned earlier in this book.

The Holy Spirit guides our intuition, builds community with us in communion, and empowers us by providing truth to our conscience to make decisions.

For God hasn't given us a spirit of fear, but a spirit of power, and of love, and of a sound mind.
- 2 TIMOTHY 1:7, NKJV

When our passion is fueled by the power, love, and sound mind of the Spirit, it is so grounded in truth, strengthened in love, and empowered by eternal guidance that it never burns out.

Through the Holy Spirit, God perfects the union of His triune being with the trinity of our Spirit and Soul.

Through the Holy Spirit, God works to be our Great Life Coach by inspiring us, encouraging us, and empowering us.

Just as these three words—inspire, encourage, and empower—serve as God's tools to ignite passion within us, they are also tools we can use to ignite passion within those around us. These tools are known as the Passioneer's Blueprints.

CHAPTER 18

THE PASSIONEER'S BLUEPRINTS

———

Therefore encourage one another and build
each other up, just as in fact you are doing.

- 1 THESSALONIANS 5:11

Back when I was in college, one of my fondest memories was being a part of the organization Bridges to Prosperity, whose mission is to end poverty in countries abroad caused by rural isolation through the development and construction of pedestrian footbridges.

In order to achieve an endeavor as ambitious as this, the most important part of the project is not only bridge construction but also the relationships developed with the community members and the empowerment that happens throughout the life of the project.

While in school, I was fortunate to have served on two bridge builds, and quite frankly, my experiences with Bridges to Prosperity have played a big role in not only shaping who I am today, but also the vision and development for some of the principles behind this book.

During my last year of college, a group of friends and I who were involved with several of the bridge builds went back to Panama for spring break to visit the communities and those who we continued to keep in touch with for several years.

The first community we visited was Caimital in the region of Cocle, Panama. The bridge constructed for this community was seventy-six meters long, but the relationships developed and the impact they had were endless.

I vividly remember the first night back in the community with my friends and Samuel. Samuel grew up in Caimital and was a young leader in the community. In fact, he played a large role along with David, the community's mason, in leading the project. If it wasn't for Samuel and David, the project may not have been as successful as it was. Samuel and David played such a critical role that they caught the attention of Bridges to Prosperity and were hired to continue empowering other communities in building pedestrian footbridges.

Our relationship with Samuel and David came full circle the following summer after the Caimital Bridge was constructed, when we returned to Panama to help another community build a footbridge. This was the community of Tucuecito. Shortly after landing in Panama, we learned both Samuel and

David would be joining us on this bridge build to together empower this community.

We reflected on our journey with Samuel and David along with Samuel during our first night back in Caimital, and I'll never forget this experience. Shortly after arriving in the community, Samuel grabbed a box of wine and some yellow plastic cups along with his phone and speaker. Samuel had a passion for music, namely American rock.

Samuel, along with my friends and some old friends in the community, made our way down Caimital's main dirt road towards the bridge.

We walked for over fifteen minutes and finally made it to the bridge. There was a lot of blood, sweat, and tears experienced during the construction of this bridge, so the level of emotion and excitement as we stepped foot on the bridge and made our way to its center was high. As the bridge bounced and swayed, we laughed about the experiences we had shared several years prior.

When we made it to the center of the bridge, we sat down. As we reminisced, Samuel put on some music by Coldplay and started to hand out the wine, and we just sat and swayed. It was so dark it felt like we were floating in the air.

While this was happening, I was so overwhelmed with emotion. As we sat and swayed on that bridge, I reflected and remembered. Of course I remembered the activities of building the bridge, but that isn't what led to the emotions bubbling up and stirring within me. It was the memories of building the relationships that lead me to be moved in a way no physical thing could ever move me.

It's so easy for us to focus on the behavior, actions, and impact, but not realize it is relationships that bring true lasting change and impact.

A PASSIONEER'S BLUEPRINTS

That moment on the bridge brought together a culmination of reflections I had for years up until that moment. It secured deep within me the conviction that a Passioneer's blueprints aren't drawings, but the souls of others. A Passioneer's blueprints are living, alive, and breathing and need to be stewarded and discipled. I remembered a Passioneer's tools aren't similar to those of typical builders, but rather the products of thoughts, words, and actions.

A Passioneer builds with the tools of inspiration, encouragement, and empowerment through the mediums of thoughts, words, and actions. Our thoughts and words carry with them so much weight. Proverbs 18:21 says the tongue has the power of life and death. And as believers and as human beings, we have a call on our lives at a minimum to build up the lives of others around us.

Furthermore, 1 Thessalonians 5:11 says, "Therefore encourage one another and build each other up, just as in fact you are doing." The original Greek word for building up here is transliterated as oikodomeó and means to literally build a house and figuratively to edify, or build, someone up.[95]

---

95   Bible Hub, s.v. "13618. oikodomeó," accessed February 22, 2021.

I was fortunate to have experienced firsthand how the tools of inspiration, encouragement, and empowerment worked in creating relationships that would in turn lead to lasting impact, so much so that after our first Bridge project in Panama, our club's motto becam, "Empowering Today, Inspirando Mañana," meaning, "Empowering Today, Inspiring Tomorrow."

A few days later while we were driving, I had an aha moment. I was reflecting deeper on the power of the words inspire, encourage, and empower and why they had such a power to not only lead others but also how the putting into action of these words impacted relationships and edified others.

I was writing out some thoughts in my journal and then came forth what I had been working through during my senior year in my own personal life. As I mentioned in Part Two of this book, I was working through a program called Restoring Relationships in which I learned about the three parts of the human soul and how it is comprised of three faculties: intellect, emotion, and will.

Pondering on the three parts of the soul and the words inspire, encourage, and empower, I gasped, and my pen could not match the enthusiasm of the ideas bubbling up within my mind. I quickly wrote empower, inspire, and encourage down in my journal and then on the same page, wrote the words intellect, emotion, and will.

As I looked at the words in my journal, I started to try and connect the dots between the words. I couldn't help but notice the relationship among them. I saw how inspire affected the mind and intellect; I saw how encourage affected emotion; I saw how empower affected the human will.

This revelation blew my mind. As I continued to work through these thoughts, I saw how inspiration affects our thoughts because our thoughts are alive and need something to pull from. You see, the word inspire comes from the Latin word inspirare, which literally means to breathe life into something.[96]

Encouragement is bringing courage into one's emotions.

Empowerment provides resources and the needs required, thus bolstering one's will and volition to make decisions.

These thoughts progressed, and as I returned home from my trip, I developed what I like to call the "Passion With Purpose" model. As you'll see in the figure below, the outermost triangle has the words inspire, encourage, and empower on it. And then the innermost triangle are the three faculties of the soul: intellect, emotion, and well. The middle triangle is the mediator between the outer and the inner. These are the functions and actions of the soul: our intellect produces thoughts, our emotions produce feelings, and our will produces choices.

96   Merriam-Webster, s.v. "Breathing Life Into 'Inspire': The word's origins are quite literal," accessed January 13, 2021.

Figure 18.1: The Passion With Purpose Model by Steven F. Mezzacappa

You see, when we inspire, encourage, and empower someone, we're not just simply doing something on the outside. We're impacting someone from the inside out.

James 1:17 says every good and perfect thing comes from above. We're going to be exposed to environments or relationships. It's up to us to understand what we take into our soul from these experiences. Think of this model as a way to filter what enters and leaves our soul in both relationships and in everyday life.

It's important to realize how our relationships with other people can affect our souls. Is this person inspiring or encouraging me? Am I empowering them?

Or when we're doing something or find ourselves in an environment, we can use this model to reflect and ask ourselves, is this behavior, action, or environment inspiring to me? Is it encouraging to me? Is it empowering to me?

When you look at the opposite of this model, we see the "Anti-Passion With Purpose" model as seen below. The opposite of inspire is expire, which takes the thoughts out of someone by introduction of negative thoughts. The opposite of encourage is discourage, and the opposite of empower is disempower.

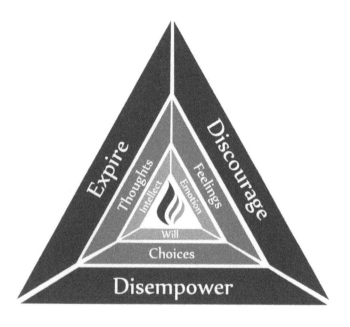

Figure 18.2: Anti-Passion With Purpose
Model by Steven F. Mezzacappa

The culmination of expire, discourage, and disempower undermine one's passion by putting it on a path to burn out, as instead of giving and pouring into the soul, these tools take away from the soul. In our relationships and environments, we should be quick to discern if relationships, actions, or environments are inspiring or expiring, encouraging or discouraging, and empowering or disempowering.

When it comes to inspiration, encouragement, and empowerment, it's all about giving and not taking. When you inspire, encourage, and empower, you are pouring into someone. You're pouring into yourself. Our souls are eternal and have eternal needs. In addition to God's spirit, we must be intentional in pouring into one another the eternal acts of inspiration, encouragement, and empowerment.

Another thing to think about is that in different seasons of life, we will need varying levels of inspiration, encouragement, and empowerment to keep our passion alive and apply it to the task or opportunity for impact at hand.

Let this book simply serve as an introduction to the Passion With Purpose model and the Passioneer's blueprints on how inspiration, encouragement, and empowerment can transform ourselves and others from the inside out.

The Passion With Purpose Model can be applied across industries, disciplines, and even in relationships; but again the application of this tool in each of these areas all deserve a book on their own.

In the next chapter, we will look closer at applying the Passion With Purpose model to the fire within and specifically, how God inspires, encourages, and empowers us by looking at the Trinity Triangle.

CHAPTER 19

THE FIRE WITHIN

———

So Moses thought, "I will go over and see this
strange sight—why the bush does not burn up."

- EXODUS 3:3

The illustration of fire is used all throughout the scriptures. From the destruction of Sodom and Gomorrah to God appearing to Moses in the burning bush in the Old Testament to the Holy Spirit coming on the Apostles like Tongues of Fire in the Book of Acts, the use of fire is consistent, intentional, and revealing.

In fact, in the book of Acts on the day of Pentecost when the Holy Spirit descended on the Apostles like "tongues of fire," the Greek word for fire used is puros, which expresses that fire is eternal. Deeper research behind the use of this word equates it with God's Spirit, which is "like a holy fire" that both "enlightens and purifies."[97] This fire empowers and

———

97   Bible Hub, s.v. "4442. pur," accessed February 22, 2021.

energizes believers to both become more like God's likeness and truly ignite fire within others.

It's easy to appreciate the use of fire as a metaphor for the Spirit of God.

FIRE AND THE HOLY SPIRIT

Fire	The Spirit of God (Holy Spirit)
Used for Light	Reveals, Teaches, and Guides
Used for Energy	Strengthens and Equips
Used for Heat	Transforms the Lives of Others

Just as literal fire illuminates, energizes, and serves, so too does the fire within you and me teach, equip, and transform our lives along with the lives of those around us.

It is this fire within us that is truly our passion. This eternal flame within us, our soul is what's breathed into us by God at conception and one day returns to Jesus in full consummation for eternity when our race is finished here on earth.

The fire within us is also contagious, felt by others around us, and is at its best truly empowering and life changing. The power of the Holy Spirit and the fire within is perhaps best demonstrated through the life and actions of Christianity's first martyr, Saint Stephen.

THE PASSION OF SAINT STEPHEN

As the Apostles envangelized and as believers continued to grow in number in the first century, there was a need for more responsible leaders. The Apostles sought to seek out seven believers who were "full of the Spirit and wisdom." One of these individuals was Stephen, believed to be a Greek Jew who converted to Christianity.[98]

Of the seven selected by the disciples to take on this leadership, Stephen was set apart in the scriptures. The other six individuals were mentioned by either name or where they were from and where they converted from, but Stephen was mentioned as, "Stephen, a man full of faith and of the Holy Spirit." When we learn about Stephen's actions and example we would rightly understand why the fire within him was intentionally mentioned.

As Stephen progressed in ministry, the Bible attributes Stephen with performing "great wonders and signs among the people." Stephen was having such a measurable and significant impact that opposition arose among Jewish leaders. Unable to stand up against "the wisdom the Spirit gave him as he spoke," Jewish leaders were led to conjure up and make a plot to seize and take Stephen captive.

Accomplishing this, Stephen was brought before the Sanhedrin. The Sanhedrin in Biblical times was the supreme council and tribunal of Jewish Leaders. The Sanhedrin was headed by a High Priest and this group maintained and executed religious, civil, and criminal jurisdiction.[99]

---

98   "Saint Stephen," *BBC*, accessed February 22, 2021.

99   Merriam-Webster, s.v. "Sanhedrin," accessed February 22, 2021.

Even before the Sanhedrin, Stephen was still exhibiting signs and fruit of the fire roaring within him. "All who were sitting in the Sanhedrin looked intently at Stephen, and they saw that his face was like the face of an angel" (Acts 6:15).

The high priest went on to ask Stephen if the charges falsely brought against him were true. Stephen was charged with speaking blasphemous words against Moses and against God.

Stephen didn't respond with a simple yes or no. Filled with the Holy Spirit, Stephen replied instead with a truth grounded and spirit-filled message regarding the liberation of the Israelites from Egypt, highlighting Old Testament passages and scripture, and confronting the Jewish leaders with truth.

The Sanhedrin's response to Stephen's message was fueled with hate and fury, something that happens when a fire fueled with love confronts a fire fueled with fear. Such a topic we will discuss deeper in the next chapter.

The Sanhedrin are accounted as gnashing their teeth at Stephen. Before long, Stephen was dragged out of the city and stoned to death.

One of the last words Stephen spoke was, "Lord, do not hold this sin against them" (Acts 7:60).

Even while undergoing a graphic death and execution, Stephen still took the time to forgive his condemners while wrongly being put to death.

How can one who is innocent and being put to death still forgive those killing him?

Stephen's passion was grounded in truth, guided by love, and strengthened by the Holy Spirit. His passion also had a purpose.

STEPHEN'S PASSION HAD PURPOSE

Throughout Stephen's actions and intense persecution, he still exhibited being full of faith, the Holy Spirit, and of wisdom while appearing to be like an angel. Even in his final moments he was forgiving.

Stephen had a clear purpose in being an ambassador for Truth and for the Gospel of Christ. He knew what he stood for and where his help, comfort, and guidance came from.

Perhaps his ability to maintain love and grace in his final moments is a testament to his full and complete reliance on God to fuel the fire he had inside of him.

Stephen, aware of his calling and the purpose God had for his life, had the impact he had because of his commitment to his identity in Christ and in what he was called to do.

In John Maxwell's Bible commentary, The Maxwell Leadership Bible, he directly attributes the leadership quality of commitment to the life and actions of Stephen. Maxwell notes Stephen "displays an unwavering commitment to his convictions."[100]

---

100 John C. Maxwell, *The Maxwell Leadership Bible, NIV* (Nashville: Thomas Nelson, 2018), 1238.

Commitment moves past the mind and emotions and goes straight to the will. The ancient Chinese said the will of a man is like a cart pulled by two horses: the mind and the emotions. You must get both horses moving in the same direction to move the cart. Commitment results when your mind and emotions move forward, whatever the cost.

- JOHN C. MAXWELL[101]

When Stephen spoke before the Sanhedrin, he didn't act based on his thoughts and feelings, but instead on his convictions through executing his volition. Stephen was empowered to act on convictions through his will even in spite of persecution and a looming execution.

Stephen was able to do this because he surrendered his will to the leading of the Holy Spirit rather than his thoughts and feelings. This also enabled God to work through Stephen.

As we discussed all throughout this book, God the Father is a great minister to our human intellect, Jesus is a great minister to our human emotion, and the Holy Spirit is a great minister to our human will.

In times of doubt, fear, uncertainty, and persecution, it is through the Holy Spirit's guidance, comfort, and equipping that we are transformed inwardly, leading to an outward impact only God can truly bring about.

Stephen's passion burned like the burning bush that appeared before Moses. The bush on fire didn't burn up, burn out, or

---

101 Ibid.

turn to soot. The fire in the bush was self-sustaining and life giving as opposed to life draining.

The fire within energy didn't drain him, but it sustained and equipped him. His fire and passion were fueled by love rather than fear.

His passion was truly fueled by the energy of the Holy Spirit.

FUELING THE FIRE WITHIN

If I were to best explain how to fuel the passion and fire within us, I would use Figure 19.1 below, The Trinity Triangle.

Figure 19.1: The Trinity Triangle by Steven F. Mezzacappa

As discussed previously and throughout this book, our soul comprises three faculties: the intellect, emotion, and will. To best breathe life into each of these faculties, thus giving life, energy, and animation to our passion—the fire within—we must feed "oxygen" into each of these faculties by way of inspiration, encouragement, and empowerment.

James 1:17 says, "Every good and perfect gift is from above, coming down from the Father of the heavenly lights, who does not change like shifting shadows."

There are things in our life that can yes, inspire us, encourage us, and empower us, but nothing can provide these needs of the soul fire within us like the breath of God's spirit, along with the Father's truth, Son's love, and Holy Spirit's guidance.

PASSION & THE SPIRIT OF GOD

In the very opening lines of the Bible, the Spirit of God is said to hover over the waters. The original Hebrew word used for God's Spirit is ruach, which is defined as breath, wind, or simply spirit.[102]

Ruach is used to describe God's personal presence because of the energy, life-giving, and vitality God's spirit provides, hence this word being defined as wind.[103]

God's Holy Spirit is again metaphorically represented as wind in the New Testament.

---

102 Bible Hub, s.v. "7307. ruach," accessed February 22, 2021.

103 *BibleProject*, "Holy Spirit," April 5, 2017, video, 4:10.

And when He had said this, He breathed on them and said to them, "Receive the Holy *Spirit*." - John 20:22 NASB

John testified saying, "I have seen the *Spirit* descending as a dove out of heaven, and He remained upon Him." - John 1:32 NASB

"As for me, I baptize you with water for repentance, but He who is coming after me is mightier than I, and I am not fit to remove His sandals; He will baptize you with the Holy *Spirit* and fire." - Matthew 3:11 NASB

In all three instances of scripture above, the Greek word used for Spirit is pneuma, which like the Hebrew word ruach, means wind, breath, and spirit.[104]

The Bible's writers were intentional in using breath and wind to describe God's Spirit because of how it gives life. In the Old Testament it was used to convey how God's Spirit sustains all life and creation. Progressing into the Old Testament ruach empowers the prophets. In the New Testament the metaphor of God's Spirit as wind is used to convey how God's Spirit "transforms the human heart, to empower people, to truly love God and others."[105]

God's Spirit fuels our passion because it breathes life into every faculty of our soul. Just like a fire requires oxygen to burn, so too does our passion—the fire within.

God's Spirit pours life into our souls by inspiring our intellect, by encouraging our emotion, and by empowering our will.

---

104 Bible Hub, s.v. "4151. pneuma," accessed February 22, 2021.

105 *BibleProject*, "Holy Spirit," April 5, 2017, video, 4:10.

If we sought to fuel our passion with the things of this world and of our carnal nature and five senses, we would have the energy to run a little while but would eventually burn out.

By solely leaning on God's ruach and pneuma, only then can we live out God's calling on our lives with a passion that never burns out.

Saint Stephen was able to accomplish what he did and especially forgive his murderers because instead of being fueled and guided by his thoughts, feelings, and physical sensations, he crucified his flesh, took up his cross, and thus leaned into his spirit, where the Holy Spirit could fully bear witness to his Spirit. Thus, the fullness of God's love, grace, goodness, comfort, and God's inspiration, encouragement, and empowerment could pour into Stephen's soul and passion and lead to the inward transformation overflowing to his demonstrated impact.

Stephen was able to have complete ownership of his passion because he was Spirit led as opposed to led by the flesh.

It is our passion that energizes us to live out our calling, but because of the fallen nature of the world we live in, our passion is prone to influence and manifestations of the viruses of sin and fear.

Such toxins seek to chart us off the course for God's plans for our lives and try to thwart our passion and burn it out.

By God's Spirit of Love, however, we have the empowerment to be fueled with love versus fear. But it remains on us if our passion is to be fueled and guided by love or to be expired and misled by fear.

CHAPTER 20

LOVE VS. FEAR

———

For God hath not given us the spirit of fear; but
of power, and of love, and of a sound mind.

- 2 TIMOTHY 1:7, KJV

Physics was definitely not my strong suit back when I was earning my degree in architectural engineering, but one thing I'll always remember from physics is that a force is defined by a push or pull upon an object.

Let's think a little more about pushes and pulls for a moment. Have you ever been out and about shopping at a grocery store or perhaps a home improvement store like Home Depot? Have you ever been browsing around with your heavy, overloaded cart and come across a busy aisle? Maybe there's a cart in the middle of the aisle with a child sitting in it while another child helps their parent find the sauce for Sunday's pasta dinner.

What would be the best way to navigate forward? Just a little behind this "roadblock" is the rigatoni you need to make dinner tonight. Your initial thought might be to turn around and go back the way you came, approaching the aisle from the other side of the store, but this would require you to go backwards, take the longer route, and perhaps encounter other roadblocks. The best path is to move forward. Like many say, there is a reason why the windshield of a car is much larger than the rearview mirror.

Progressing forward, the next thought is to push your cart forward from behind where the handles are, but with the cart being so heavy, you don't have much control to stop once the cart gets moving. It's also much more challenging to steer the cart from behind to direct it and navigate through the roadblocks.

You resort to elect the best option: jumping to the front of the cart and navigating through the roadblock while pulling the cart behind you. In pulling the cart, you have more control to lead where the cart goes.

At the end of the day, as the expression goes, the horse came before the cart.

Such an illustration is important to take note of when we look at the forces of love and fear and their influence on our soul and passion.

LOVE VS. FEAR

If we were to associate love and fear with the forces of pushing and pulling, love can be characterized as a pull, or drawing nature, and fear can be characterized as a push, or driving nature.

Throughout our lives, and on a constant basis, our souls are influenced to be drawn by love or driven by fear. Through sin, struggle, and strife along with unreconciled pain within our hearts, it is an ongoing battle for our will and volition to be drawn or driven.

Scripture is clear in guiding us to be led by love and not by fear. 2 Timothy 1:7 (KJV) says, "For God hath not given us the spirit of fear; but of power, and of love, and of a sound mind."

Let's dive deeper into this verse for a moment and look closer at the original Greek words used in the text for spirit, fear, power, love, and sound mind.

Spirit - Pneuma, as detailed in the previous chapter, is used to express not simply an external spirit or influential force, but the divine Spirit of God and His Holy Spirit. God is love (1 John 4:7–21 NIV).

Fear - Deilia, specifically means cowardice, timidity, reticence and roots. It originates from the Greek word deilos,[106] which refers to a dreadful fear "describing a person who loses the 'moral gumption (fortitude)' that is needed to follow the Lord."[107]

Power - Dunamis, is used to express a power, might, or strength that is miraculous,[108] and stems from the Greek

---

106 Bible Hub, s.v. "1167. deilia," accessed February 23, 2021.

107 Bible Hub, s.v. "1169. deilos," accessed February 23, 2021.

108 Bible Hub, s.v. "1411. dunamis," accessed February 23, 2021.

word dunamai, that is a power "enabled by God" and in essence demonstrates God's true empowerment of us.[109]

Love - Agape, as detailed in a previous chapter, is a word for sacrificial and selfless love. It is divine love in the fullest and is best evident in what Christ did on the cross.

Sound Mind - Sóphronismos, specifically means self-control, self-discipline, and prudence.[110] It is derived from the Greek word sophron, which means "acting in God's definition of balance." It is used to express a God-defined balance and describes "a man who does not command himself, but rather is commanded by God." Digging a little deeper, the root phrēn in this word "is the root of 'diaphram,' the inner organ (muscle) that regulates physical life, controlling breathing and heart beat" while the root sōphro- "comes from sōos ('safe')".[111] Together, the sound mind we receive from God is this safe life-leading regulation.

The Divine Spirit of God that resides alongside our spirit is not one of reticence, passivity, or timidity; the Spirit of God that dwells within us is the epitome of spiritual empowerment, the quintessence of sacrificial love, and the personification of divinely balanced discipline.

Such a Spirit is one that is essential to fuel our passions, not simply for our benefit alone, but also the benefit of others around us.

---

109 Bible Hub, s.v. "1410. dunamai," accessed February 23, 2021.

110 Bible Hub, s.v. "4995. sóphronismos," accessed February 23, 2021.

111 Bible Hub, s.v. "4998. sóphrón," accessed February 23, 2021.

Passion is often associated with charisma not only because of the enthusiasm exhibited by one, but also because of how one feels around a passionate person.

People will forget what you said, people will forget what you did, but people will never forget how you made them feel.
- MAYA ANGELOU[112]

When we ground our passion in the Spirit of God's love as opposed to the enemy's Spirit of fear, our passion is fueled by and bears the fruits of the Holy Spirit, which include: love, joy, peace, forbearance, kindness, goodness, faithfulness, gentleness, and self-control (Galatians 5:22–23).

It is the passion bearing this fruit that truly leads to transformation and the empowerment to make an impact without risk of burnout.

Each moment of each day we have the decision to either let love or fear steward and cultivate our passion. Interestingly enough, the very verse presiding 2 Timothy 1:7 reads, "For this reason I remind you to fan into flame the gift of God, which is in you through the laying on of my hands" (2 Timothy 1:6).

Friends, when the enemy tries to extinguish the passion within us through the spirit of fear and through sin and life's struggles and strife, choose to fan love into the fire of your passion. Choose God. Choose life (Deuteronomy 30:19).

---

112 "Maya Angelou > Quotes > Quotable Quote," Goodreads, accessed January 13, 2021.

There is no fear in love. But perfect love drives out fear, because fear has to do with punishment. The one who fears is not made perfect in love.

- 1 JOHN 4:18

As good and evil wage war in the world, so too does the battle between love and fear rage to take ownership of our passion; but when it comes to love and fear, there isn't as much of a gray line as one might imagine. The distinction between love and fear is quite clear.

LOVE VS. FEAR

Love	Fear
Pulls	Pushes
Draws	Drives
Gives Liberty	Takes Captive
Gentle	Forceful
Inspires	Expires
Encourages	Discourages
Empowers	Disempowers

We want to live with a passion that empowers us to think, feel, and choose with things that are lovely and pure. "Finally, brothers and sisters, whatever is true, whatever is noble, whatever is right, whatever is pure, whatever is lovely, whatever is admirable—if anything is excellent or praiseworthy—think about such things" (Philippians 4:8).

When our passion is fueled by love, it sustains spiritual self, while edifying those around us. When our passion is filled with fear, it extinguishes our spiritual self and "burns" those around us, expiring their passion.

The question we must ponder continuously when taking self-inventory is, "Are we being driven by fear or drawn by love?"

There are times when it can be difficult to discern whether our passion is grounded in love or rooted in fear. As discussed earlier in this book, a passion grounded and fueled by love is soulical passion while a passion filled and overridden with fear is a soulish passion.

To simplify this metaphor, I use the illustration of blue passion and red passion. I visualize passion on a spectrum based on how it burns by metaphorically looking at its color as seen in Figure 20.1 below. Because this book is not printed in color, please take note the darker grey flame in Figure 20.1 corresponds with a red passion, while the lighter gray flame corresponds with a blue passion.

Figure 20.1 The Fire Within Spectrum by Steven F. Mezzacappa

The white flame (furthest left) represents a consecrated passion that is purely soulical and under the guidance of God. The black flame (furthest right) represents a deconsecrated passion that is fully soulish and dominated by the enemy's spirit of fear. Ultimately, the white flame represents complete life of passion, while the black flame represents complete death of passion.

Since these are the extreme ends of the spectrum, we should focus our attention on the blue (light gray) and red (dark gray) flames. A blue flame represents soulical passion sustained by love and a red flame represents soulish passion dominated by fear.

To best illustrate the differences between these two, let's look at the fruit each feeds us and then the fruit each bears to others around us.

SOULICAL PASSION (LOVE) VS. SOULISH PASSION (FEAR)

IMPACTS ON SELF

Soulical Passion (Love)	Soulish Passion (Fear)
Sustaining	Draining
Controllable	Uncontrollable
Disciplined	Impulsive
Conscious	Unconscious
Drawn by Love	Driven by Pain
Freeing	Dominating
Balanced & Directed	Unbalanced & lacks Direction

SOULICAL PASSION (LOVE) VS. SOULISH PASSION (FEAR)

IMPACTS ON OTHERS

Soulical Passion (Love)	Soulish Passion (Fear)
Ignites Energy	Expires Energy
Empowering	Controlling
Gives Liberty	Takes Captive
Joyful	Anxious
Gives	Takes Away
Edifies	Tears Down
Loves Sacrificially	"Loves" with Ulterior Motives

The above tables are meant to serve as an introduction to this topic, as a whole series of books can be written going into the deep psychology and spiritual influences of soulical and soulish passion. There are aspects that are clear, conscious, and obvious and other cases where it is unclear, unconscious, and not so obvious.

To provide a personal example, when I achieved what I had in college, the passion that motivated me to be accomplished was soulish at its best. By the end of college, I was burnt out and insecure in my most precious relationships, filled with despair, anxious, and lacked life direction. Though successful in the eyes of the world, I felt like someone who had gained the whole world but who had lost their soul (Mark 8:36 NLT).

Not only was I "burnt" by my own passion, but I also hurt, or "burnt," some of those closest to me unintentionally. This concept of soulical and soulish passion can be difficult to discern at times, but for the time being in this book, it's my hope to empower you in this discernment process by encouraging you to take your thoughts and questions before the Lord and seek His counsel with two specific questions: What is my relationship with God like and what is my relationship like with those around me, specifically the most precious people in my life?

Ask God: How is my relationship with you Lord? Do I seek you out? Do I praise you? Do I trust you?

Ask God: How is my relationship with others? Am I easily offended? Do I freely give to others without ulterior motives?

A healthy relationship with both God and others can serve as a baseline for a healthy soulical passion fueled by love, while an unhealthy relationship with God coupled with toxic relationships with others can serve as an indicator of a soulish passion residing within, filled with and dominated by fear.

When it comes to love and fear, we should not seek balance between the two. We must earnestly seek out love, and not simply the kind of love defined by basic English. We should passionately seek out the love that the white flame truly represents—agape—the love perfectly demonstrated and freely given to us by the Great Architect, the Great Physician, and the Great Life Coach.

It is by flooding our souls with the love of our Father that we can truly impact the lives of others around us by demonstrating agape in its fullest and by edifying others around us (Romans 5:5).

Therefore, since we are surrounded by such a great cloud of witnesses, let us throw off everything that hinders and the sin that so easily entangles. And let us run with perseverance the race marked out for us, fixing our eyes on Jesus, the pioneer and perfecter of faith. For the joy set before him he endured the cross, scorning its shame, and sat down at the right hand of the throne of God. Consider him who endured such opposition from sinners, so that you will not grow weary and lose heart.

- HEBREWS 12:1–3

CHAPTER 21

IMPACT – BEING
A PASSIONEER

———

*Their work will be shown for what it is, because the Day
will bring it to light. It will be revealed with fire, and the
fire will test the quality of each person's work. If what has
been built survives, the builder will receive a reward. If
it is burned up, the builder will suffer loss but yet will be
saved—even though only as one escaping through the flames.*

- 1 CORINTHIANS 3:13–15

If one day the money made from your work or the goods, services,
and activities produced from your endeavors all faded away,
would you still do what you do? Why do you do what you do
each day? Even if you are a student, a caretaker, a friend, or a
parent, why do you get out of bed each day? Is it to achieve? Is it
to simply experience life and enjoy it? Or is it to make an impact?

I think it's easy to associate achievement with making an
impact or to associate impact with economically or even

medically empowering someone. Of course, these areas make a difference, but when it comes to making an impact by being a Passioneer and Child of God, true impact is measured in light of eternity as opposed to the timeline and parameters of life on Earth.

The opening verse of this chapter discusses how a fire will test the quality and measure of our work. If it survives the fire, it is demonstrated success, but if it does not survive the fire and burns away, it is not so successful.

When I reflect on these verses, I think of legacy and demonstrated impact. Working in construction management, it is easy to stand in awe and wonder at the magnificent buildings and projects I have been a part of, but not only will I not be present here one day, but these buildings will not be present here either.

When my race of life on Earth is complete, there is one thing that will remain forever, however—the impact I have made on the souls of those around me.

Then we will no longer be infants, tossed back and forth by the waves, and blown here and there by every wind of teaching and by the cunning and craftiness of people in their deceitful scheming. Instead, speaking the truth in love, we will grow to become in every respect the mature body of him who is the head, that is, Christ. From Him the whole body, joined and held together by every supporting ligament, grows and builds itself up in love, as each part does its work.

- EPHESIANS 4:14–16

I ask myself and will ask you the same question: how much time and effort do I invest in building others up in love by speaking the truth in love?

Impact is not measured by how much we physically provide, but by how much we love. Our passion does not need money to thrive. Our passion does not need glory to flourish. Our passion does not need materialistic success to be demonstrated. Such devices would only lead to a soulish passion anyway.

Our passion—our soul—the fire within you and I, simply needs divine truth, divine love, and divine guidance.

So Christ himself gave the apostles, the prophets, the evangelists, the pastors and teachers, to equip his people for works of service, so that the body of Christ may be built up until we all reach unity in the faith and in the knowledge of the Son of God and become mature attaining to the whole measure of the fullness of Christ.
                                    - EPHESIANS 4:11-13 (NIV)

God edifies His people by using apostles, prophets, evangelists, pastors, and teachers to equip us with a passion grounded in truth and in love to truly fulfill our callings in life so we may experience the fullness of Christ and make His love known to others as well.

Our calls to make an impact have not so much to do with us, but truly have to do with the hearts of others around us. Perhaps our level of impact can be measured upon how intentional we are in passioneering the lives of others around us.

Rather than making one's life more empowering through goods, services, or programs, we should ask ourselves if we are also empowering them internally as much as we are externally.

All external transformations will fade away one day, but the transformation that takes place within the hearts and minds of people is what lasts forever.

Such an endeavor is not dependent on one's personality or skill or level of education or certifications. All one truly needs to make a demonstrated impact in the life of another is to know God and know His love (1 John 4:7). It is important that we continually seek to grow in our relationship with God, but do not be mistaken—doing and achieving does not lead to more love. It is in "being" and in being authentic that we find love.

There are many forms and definitions that exist to describe influence, impact, and leadership, but there is one form of leadership that truly speaks to the idea of impact through love: transformational leadership.

John C. Maxwell defines transformational leadership this way:

Transformational leadership influences people to think, speak, and act in such a way that it makes a positive difference in their life and in the lives of others.

- JOHN C. MAXWELL[113]

113 John Maxwell and Mark Cole, "Transformational Leadership (Part 1)," February 3, 2021, in *The John Maxwell Leadership Podcast*, produced by John C. Maxwell, podcast, MP3 audio, 34:58.

Take note of the words used by Maxwell above: think, speak, and act. Each of these three stem from each of the soul's three faculties. Our intellect produces thoughts. Our emotion leads to what we speak. Our will produces choices, actions, and behaviors.

When we take on the call to love others and embody the principle of transformational leadership, we make an eternal imprint within the souls of those around us. It is the imprints within our souls that last forever, and while running our race on earth, these imprints have the ability to ignite our passion or drain our passion.

By being Passioneers and by taking on this call to action, it is by being grounded in the Great Architect's divine truth, the Great Physician's divine love, and the Great Life Coach's divine guidance that we can truly weather the storms of life and the enemy's cunning deceit to not let anything hold us back in truly loving others and pouring inspiration, encouragement, and empowerment into every piece of their soul.

We should seek to not simply live a life, but build a life. We should build up each other's passions so that not only one's relationship with Christ comes to fullness, but also who they were created to be comes to fullness.

To build up and edify the lives of others around us, we should take on the honorable call of being a Passioneer—one who ignites passion in others through the divine tools of inspiration, encouragement, and empowerment.

We must inspire as God the Father inspires us. We must encourage as God the Son encourages us. We must empower as God the Holy Spirit empowers us.

We must build upward our understanding of who God says He is. We must build inward by letting Jesus into the deepest and most precious areas of our heart. We must build outward by being filled, equipped, and fueled by the Holy Spirit.

We must continually fan into flame the gift of God which is in us through the love we provide to one another (2 Timothy 1:6).

What is a life worth living if we haven't impacted one's intellect, emotion, and will along the way? One day all we materially possess will fade away, but the impact we have made in the souls of those around us will surely live forever.

Be a Passioneer in everything God has called you to do, so that one day you can write as the Apostle Paul writes, "I have fought the good fight, I have finished the race, I have kept the faith" (2 Timothy 4:7).

As a prisoner for the Lord, then, I urge you to live a life worthy of the calling you have received. Be completely humble and gentle; be patient, bearing with one another in love. Make every effort to keep the unity of the Spirit through the bond of peace. There is one body and one Spirit, just as you were called to one hope when you were called; one Lord, one faith, one baptism; one God and Father of all, who is over all and through all and in all.

- EPHESIANS 4:1-6

END MATTER

FINAL CHARGE

———

For we are God's handiwork, created in Christ Jesus to do
good works, which God prepared in advance for us to do.

- EPHESIANS 2:10

When I was in the middle of writing this book, I sat down
with Pastor Ed Glover, the founder of the Urban Impact
Foundation in Pittsburgh, Pennsylvania, to seek his Godly
counsel and wisdom regarding this book and all God has
revealed to my Spirit regarding my calling in life.

There is something truly intimate about sharing your deepest
thoughts and revelations with another when your intellect
is still trying to catch up with what God has revealed and
communicated to your spirit.

I took away a lot from that conversation, but two things will
forever stand out: the call to be obedient to God's call and
three questions to ponder daily throughout the journey when
discerning and living out your calling.

Pastor Ed affirmed my calling to write this book and that I should not let anything stop me from carrying out this endeavor no matter what. The power of this encouragement, though, was that I needed to write this book not because of the potential impact or outcome it can have, but solely because God called me to write it. To have this vision and calling and not carry it out would simply go against God's will.

"If anyone, then, knows the good they ought to do and doesn't do it, it is sin for them."

- JAMES 4:17

He then shared with me the three elements of a call,—burden, vision, and joy—by slipping me a piece of paper that had three powerful questions on it.

1. What do I weep about? Burden—what burdens me?

2. What do I dream about? Vision—what's my vision?

3. What do I sing about? Joy—what gives me real joy?

I wanted to quit and give up on writing this book many times, admittedly. It felt more like a wrestling match than an opportunity to restfully sit in a coffee shop listening to jazz and sipping on coffee. But the burden within me far outweighed the spiritual opposition.

Daily I carry within my soul a spiritual burden when I see how the devastation of a broken heart leads to more pain, turmoil, and chaos in this world, in addition to the missed opportunities for those reaching the fullness of who they are in Christ and in who they were created and called to be.

Motivational speaker Les Brown often says the richest place on Earth is the graveyard because all the dreams that were never fulfilled are laid to rest there.[114] Our time here on Earth is limited, and one of the biggest things holding us back from a deeper, more intimate relationship with God and His calling in our life is a hurting heart with broken passion.

I cannot help but dream of people fueling their passion with the divine truth of God, the divine love of Jesus, and the divine guidance of the Holy Spirit. When I dream of this, I see unity, peace, and true change in the world. I see people worshiping God, loving people, and fulfilling who they were created to be and called to do.

These burdens and visions are daily for me, but I only believe so because of the joy I feel in my soul when I ponder this vision coming alive along with the joy of the Lord I experience deeply in my Spirit.

What greater joy exists than to know the Creator of the universe and all things seen and unseen set you and me apart from all of Creation, made us in His image, and despite our shortcomings, He sacrificed His one and only son so we may share in eternal life with Him one day and receive the gift of the Holy Spirit while running our race here on Earth.

---

114 "Les Brown > Quotes > Quotable Quote," Goodreads, accessed January 13, 2021.

I urge you to move forward in life not finding joy alone in your passions, gifts, talents, or even callings. From the bottom of my soul, I charge you to move forward in life with a passion ignited, fueled, and sustained by the joy of Christ that resides deep within you.

Building passion, answering the call from Christ, and living out what you are called to do can often require seasons of pain, despair, loneliness, rejection, and immense suffering within the spiritual realm. The temporal things of this world along with your talents won't be what carry you through. It will be Jesus who carries you and sustains you.

No matter what happens to us along our journey in life, Christ is enough. Do not be fooled by the title of this book. A life of fulfillment, destiny, and impact has nothing to do with personal wealth, glory, and achievement, and everything to do with Jesus Christ.

When the love of Jesus ignites, fuels, and sustains the fire within you, this is what it means to experience and build a life of fulfillment, destiny, and impact. With Jesus at the core of our identity, this is how we truly and authentically answer the questions of what makes us weep, dream, and sing.

Friends, let us together inspire one another, encourage one another, and empower one another as we do what Jesus has called us to do: deny ourselves, take up our cross daily, and follow Him (Luke 9:23).

The Preeminence of Christ

He is the image of the invisible God, the firstborn of all creation. For by him all things were created, in heaven and on earth, visible and invisible, whether thrones or dominions or rulers or authorities—all things were created through him and for him. And he is before all things, and in him all things hold together. And he is the head of the body, the church. He is the beginning, the firstborn from the dead, that in everything he might be preeminent. For in him all the fullness of God was pleased to dwell, and through him to reconcile to himself all things, whether on earth or in heaven, making peace by the blood of his cross.

And you, who once were alienated and hostile in mind, doing evil deeds, he has now reconciled in his body of flesh by his death, in order to present you holy and blameless and above reproach before him, if indeed you continue in the faith, stable and steadfast, not shifting from the hope of the gospel that you heard, which has been proclaimed in all creation under heaven, and of which I, Paul, became a minister.

- COLOSSIANS 1:15–23, ESV

NEXT STEPS

———

The message and vision for Passion With Purpose far extends this book. From online social media communities to student and professional organizations, visit www.passionwithpurpose.life and click on the "Be a Passioneer" tab to learn more.

If you would like to connect with Steven F. Mezzacappa personally, you can email him at steven@passionwithpurpose.life.

REFLECTION QUESTIONS

———

CHAPTER 1: DON'T FOLLOW YOUR PASSION

1. What was your initial response to the phrase: Don't Follow Your Passion?

2. Before reading this chapter, what was your definition of passion?

3. How would you define soulical passion and soulish passion in your own words?

4. Can you think of a time when God has led you to do something that required seasons of adversity or internal turmoil?

5. In what areas of your life do you follow passion and in what other areas do you build passion?

6. How would you define and describe divine truth, divine love, and divine guidance?

CHAPTER 2: BUILD YOUR PASSION

1. Can you think of a time in your life when you worked off of a "faulty" foundation? What were the impacts and results?

2. How can you apply the relationship of the spirit and soul to your life?

3. How can you build up your passion from the Spirit as opposed to the Body?

4. What are some of the ways in which we build up our passion from the Body that may undermine our passion?

5. What role does Free Will play in building passion?

6. What is presently influencing your soul more right now? What percentage would you assign to the Spirit and Body influencing your soul? (e.g., 45 percent Spirit, 55 percent Body)

CHAPTER 3: THE GREAT ARCHITECT & HIS BLUEPRINTS

1. How much authority do you give the Word of God over your life?

2. How would you define humility?

3. Reflect on a time when you or someone demonstrated humility.

4. Why is it important to approach the Word of God with a humble heart?

5. How would you further distinguish the difference between culture's blueprints and God's blueprints for a fulfilling life?

6. How does the current culture you live in define fulfillment? How does God define fulfillment?

CHAPTER 4: THE PASSION OF THE IMAGO DEI

1. What do you think it means to be created in the image of God?

2. Reflect on and/or discuss other stories where we see Jesus exercising His intellect.

3. Reflect on and/or discuss other stories where we see Jesus exercising His emotion.

4. Reflect on and/or discuss other stories where we see Jesus exercising His will/volition.

5. How can we steward our passion in a way that allows others see the Image of God in us?

6. What other comparisons can you draw between fire and passion?

CHAPTER 5: WHY DO WE STRUGGLE?

1. What would you describe as the characteristics of struggle?

2. Is struggle something you seek to avoid or embrace?

3. Have you ever had an experience similar to Job where you struggled and suffered without a clear reason?

4. How has any struggle you have faced or any struggles faced by individuals you may know had an impact on you?

5. Taking inspiration from C. S. Lewis's quote, "God whispers to us in our pleasures, speaks in our conscience, but shouts in our pains," have you ever had an experience where God revealed to you something through your pain?

CHAPTER 6: WAR, WRESTLING, & PASSION

1. Of all the places to wage war on Believers, why do you think the enemy attacks the human mind?

2. How can we apply the full armor of God (Ephesians 6:10–17) to our lives?

3. How do you think Spiritual Warfare undermines our passion?

CHAPTER 7: FULFILLMENT—WINNING THE WAR ON PASSION

1. How would you describe winning the war on passion in your own words?

2. To what degree do you live your life in the moment in comparison to living your life for the future?

3. How can you live in the moment daily?

4. What is the present definition you have for fulfillment that grounds your perspective on what it means to have a fulfilling life?

5. When and how did you first define success and fulfillment? Who/what influences your perspective of fulfillment?

CHAPTER 8: JOBS, CAREERS, CALLINGS, & PURPOSE

1. How would you differentiate jobs, careers, and callings?

2. How do you define purpose in your own life?

3. On a scale of one to ten (one being the lowest, ten being the highest), how would you rank the confidence you have in your calling and purpose in life? Share/journal the reason why for your answer.

4. Why do you think it is necessary to have a relationship with Jesus in order to discern our callings in life?

5. What do you think it means to "remain" in Jesus's love, as described in John 15:9?

CHAPTER 9: PURPOSE VS. DESTINY

1. What makes you feel valued and significant?

2. How would you describe the difference between purpose and destiny?

3. Have you ever had an opportunity to make an impact that was not planned, but brought about by God?

4. Do you view purpose as something large-scale and significant or something as simple as empathizing with a friend?

5. How can we live more presently and be aware of the divine appointments God makes in our lives to have purpose?

6. What are some of the spiritual gifts you think God has blessed you with? If nothing comes to mind right away, spend some time in prayer and journal your conversation with God. If in a group setting, spend some time affirming one another's spiritual gifts by identifying the gifting you see in one another.

CHAPTER 10: THE PASSION OF SALVATION

1. How would you describe the functions of the soul without influence from the Spirit?

2. How would you define the differences between justice, mercy, and grace in your own words?

3. How can we experience salvation now?

4. How would you express the relationship between salvation and passion in your own words?

CHAPTER 11: KNOWING YOUR IDENTITY

1. Why do you think some find it challenging to be truly authentic?

2. How would you define identity in your own words?

3. Discuss or journal about what we do being simply an application of our identity as opposed to being solely our identity.

4. Which of Peter Scazzero's three false identities do you find challenge you the most? Performance-based (I am What I Do), Possession-based (I am What I Have), Popularity-based (I Am What Others Think)

5. How and why does having an identity in Christ ignite, fuel, and sustain our passion?

CHAPTER 12: PASSION, PURPOSE, & THE INFECTED SOUL

1. Reflect and meditate on Proverbs 4:23 (AMP), "Watch over your heart with all diligence, For from it flow the springs of life." Discuss and/or journal your convictions regarding this verse.

2. How do you think one can discern if the present struggles in their life are related to a soul infection manifested from previous emotional trauma?

3. How do you think an infected soul can undermine one's passion?

4. How do you think an infected soul can compromise God's callings in our lives?

CHAPTER 13: FORGIVENESS, RECONCILIATION, & PASSION

1. Why do you think it is sometimes difficult to forgive?

2. Why are we sometimes tempted to repress an offense instead of confronting it?

3. Aside from what's discussed in this chapter, how else do you think the sin of unforgiveness affects us and our passion?

4. How does one discern if they've truly and volitionally forgiven someone?

5. How can we be made aware and discern whether we unknowingly have unforgiveness within our hearts?

CHAPTER 14: DESTINY - THE PURPOSE OF YOUR PASSION

1. How would you describe the difference between a dream and a calling in your own words?

2. Why do you think Jesus tells us, "we must deny ourselves and take up our cross daily" in order to truly follow Him?

3. How would you further describe what the purpose of your passion is as it relates to fulfillment and destiny?

4. How would you further describe the role our passion plays in living out our purpose?

CHAPTER 15: THE ART OF PASSIONEERING

1. Describe your familiarity with the terms evangelism, discipleship, and edification.

2. Describe your experiences with evangelism, discipleship, and edification. Have you provided these

experiences to others? How can you evangelize, discipline, and edify those around you daily?

3. Do you currently have a Spiritual mentor? If not, what is the very next step you can make to have a mentor?

4. Take some time to reflect and identify anything in your life that may be hindering your passion. Reflect on the sections: Sin, Good vs. Evil, and Self in this chapter as a starting point.

5. Describe/share Passioneering in your own words. In what areas of our life can we apply this principle to edify ourselves and others around us?

CHAPTER 16: OWNING YOUR STRUGGLES

1. How would you define the difference among sin, soul struggles, and bad habits?

2. How can one utilize their intellect, emotion, and will to own their struggle?

3. Why do you think it is easy for one to make their struggle their identity?

4. Are there any biblical figures who have struggled that you can identify with?

5. How is God's strength made perfect in our weakness? (2 Corinthians 12:9)

6. What role does the human will play in building up our passion?>

CHAPTER 17: THE HOLY SPIRIT & YOU

1. Have you ever paused to take self-inventory and ask yourself why you do the things you do? Are you searching something or someone out? Are you trying to be comforted? Are you seeking guidance or counsel? Are you seeking an advocate?

2. Journal/share how the Holy Spirit can inspire, encourage, and empower you.

3. Is there anyone in your life that operates as an "advocate" as the Holy Spirit is defined by? What can you learn from this relationship that can help you understand your relationship with the Holy Spirit more?

4. How often do you quiet yourself and unplug to listen to the guidance and leading of the Holy Spirit?

5. In what areas of your life do you desire for the Holy Spirit to be your Great Life Coach? Have you asked for His guidance and support?

CHAPTER 18: THE PASSIONEER'S BLUEPRINTS

1. What do relationships mean to you when it comes to making an impact?

2. In what ways can you edify others around you more often?

3. How do you spend your time outside of your daily responsibilities? What are some of the things you do, entertain yourself with, and what environments do you typically find yourself in? Are these items/areas more relevant to the Passion With Purpose model or the Anti-Passion With Purpose model?

4. What are some things you can introduce more often into your life that are inspiring, encouraging, or empowering?

5. What are some things you can remove from your life that are expiring, discouraging, or disempowering?

CHAPTER 19: THE FIRE WITHIN

1. Journal/share how the Holy Spirit may have guided you, strengthened you, or transformed you throughout your life.

2. Reflect on some of the qualities of Saint Stephen. In what areas can you relate to him, and in what areas can you learn from him and his leadership?

3. This chapter shared a quote by John C. Maxwell that said, "Commitment results when your mind and emotions move forward, whatever the cost." Can you think of a time in your life when you stayed committed regardless of what your feelings were telling you?

4. How would you define the difference between conviction and emotions in your own words?

5. Mediate on The Trinity Triangle. In what ways can you go deeper in your relationship with God so you can allow Him to further inspire, encourage, and empower you?

CHAPTER 20: LOVE VS. FEAR

1. Journal/Share experiences when you felt drawn by love and driven by fear. Compare and contrast these experiences.

2. How would you describe the difference between love and fear in your own words?

3. How does the enemy utilize fear to undermine our passion?

4. How does God use love to inspire, encourage, and empower our passion?

5. Where does your passion presently lie on The Fire Within spectrum in Figure 20.1? What can you do to make your passion burn increasingly with blue flames and toward a white flame?

6. Assess your passion based on the distinctions made in the table showing the differences between soulical passion and soulish passion. Is your passion presently trending towards being soulical or soulish?

7. Take some time alone and quietly seek the Lord on the two following questions:

    a. How is my relationship with you Lord?

b. Lord, how is my relationship with others?

CHAPTER 21: IMPACT - BEING A PASSIONEER

1. Can you identify "apostles, prophets, evangelists, pastors, and teachers" presently in your life who are "Passioneering" your relationship with God?

2. What are some ways you can embody and apply transformational leadership principles in your life?

3. In what ways can you be a "Passioneer" for others in your life?

4. What are some of the impacts you desire to have in this life that will survive the testing by fire as described in 1 Corinthians 3:13–15?

APPENDIX

———

INTRODUCTION

Nee, Watchman. The Spiritual Man. New York: Christian Fellowship Publishers, Inc, 1977.

CHAPTER 1: DON'T FOLLOW YOUR PASSION

Affordable Colleges Online. "Depression & College Students." Accessed January 13, 2021.
https://www.affordablecollegesonline.org/college-resource-center/college-student-depression/.

Anxiety and Depression Association of America. "Facts & Statistics." Accessed January 13, 2021.
https://adaa.org/about-adaa/press-room/facts-statistics.

Beck Institute for Cognitive Behavior Therapy. "Cognitive Model." Accessed January 13, 2021.
https://beckinstitute.org/cognitive-model/#:~:text=A%20thought%20process%20for%20developing,(and%20often%20physiological)%20reactions.

Bible Hub. "1 Thessalonians 5:23." Bible Hub. Accessed January 13, 2021.
https://biblehub.com/lexicon/1_thessalonians/5-23.htm

Bible Hub. "5590. psuche." Bible Hub. Accessed January 13, 2021.
https://biblehub.com/greek/5590.htm.

Centers for Disease Control and Prevention. "Increase in Suicide Mortality in the United States, 1999–2018." Accessed January 13, 2021.
https://www.cdc.gov/nchs/products/databriefs/db362.htm.

Kelly, Jack. "More Than Half of U.S. Workers Are Unhappy In Their Jobs: Here's Why And What Needs To Be Done Now." Forbes, October 25, 2019.
https://www.forbes.com/sites/jackkelly/2019/10/25/more-than-half-of-us-workers-are-unhappy-in-their-jobs-heres-why-and-what-needs-to-be-done-now/?sh=7b93ae692024.

Maxwell, John, and Mark Cole. "Transformational Leadership (Part 1)." February 3, 2021. In The John Maxwell Leadership Podcast. Produced by John C. Maxwell. Podcast, MP3 audio, 34:58.
https://open.spotify.com/episode/7EK3W4490UrDgJehyDmeK4.

Mental Health America. "Depression in The Workplace." Accessed January 13, 2021.
https://www.mhanational.org/depression-workplace.

Mental Health America. "Mental Health in America - Printed Reports." Accessed January 13, 2021.
https://mhanational.org/issues/mental-health-america-printed-reports.

Nee, Watchman. The Spiritual Man. New York: Christian Fellowship Publishers, Inc, 1977.

Online Etymology Dictionary. s.v. "passion (n.)." Online Etymology Dictionary. Accessed January 13, 2021.
https://www.etymonline.com/word/passion.

Online Etymology Dictionary. s.v. "psychology (n.)." Online Etymology Dictionary. Accessed January 13, 2021.
https://www.etymonline.com/word/passion.

Rolheiser, Ronald. The Passion and the Cross. Cincinnati: Franciscan Media, 2015.

Therapist Aid. "The Cognitive Behavioral Model." Accessed January 13, 2021.
https://www.therapistaid.com/therapy-worksheet/cognitive-behavioral-model.

CHAPTER 2: BUILD YOUR PASSION

Leaf, Caroline. Switch On Your Brain: The Key to Peak Happiness, Thinking, and Health. Grand Rapids: Baker Publishing Group, 2015.

Lumen Learning. "Introduction to the Field of Psychology." Accessed January 13, 2021.
https://courses.lumenlearning.com/boundless-psychology/chapter/introduction-to-the-field-of-psychology/#:~:text=The%20late%2019th%20century%20marked,to%20psychological%20research%20in%20Leipzig.

Nee, Watchman. The Spiritual Man. New York: Christian Fellowship Publishers, Inc, 1977.

Rev. Clarence Larkin Estate. "Charts by Rev. Clarence Larkin - The Threefold Nature of Man." Accessed January 13, 2021.
http://www.larkinestate.com/charts.html.

CHAPTER 3: THE GREAT ARCHITECT & HIS BLUEPRINTS

Atlas Obscura. "Tuned Mass Damper of Taipei 101." Accessed January 14, 2021.
https://www.atlasobscura.com/places/tuned-mass-damper-of-taipei-101#:~:text=Inside%20the%20Taipei%20101%20skyscraper,motion%20of%20the%20building%20itself.&text=The%20Taipei%20101%20Tuned%20Mass,tested%20by%20A%26H%20Custom%20Machine.

Bible Hub. s.v. "4240. prautes." Bible Hub. Accessed January 14, 2021.
https://biblehub.com/greek/4240.htm.

McEneaney, Ciaran. Culture Trip (blog). "A Brief History of Taiwan's Taipei 101."
January 8, 2019. Accessed January 14, 2021.
https://theculturetrip.com/asia/taiwan/articles/a-brief-history-of-taiwans-taipei-101/.

CHAPTER 4: THE PASSION OF THE IMAGO DEI

Bishop Robert Barron. "How to Lose Your Soul (And How to Save It) — Bishop
Barron's Sunday Sermon." August 30, 2020. Video, 17:09.
https://www.youtube.com/watch?v=6dmL48CUdWg&ab_
channel=BishopRobertBarron.

Christianity.com. "What Does "Imago Dei" Mean? The Image of God in the Bible."
Accessed January 14, 2021.
https://www.christianity.com/wiki/bible/image-of-god-meaning-imago-dei-in-the-
bible.html.

EnigmaChurch. "Imago Dei: The Basis for Human Rights (Voddie Baucham)," May
20, 2009. Video, 8:11.
https://www.youtube.com/watch?v=rDTpDRyhtyU&list=PL06dxQJJXULeCCguNp
jcKozLwrvTADaTH&index=3&ab_channel=EnigmaChurch.

Graff, Frank. UNC-TV (blog). "How Many Daily Decisions Do We Make?."
February 7, 2018. Accessed January 14, 2021.
http://science.unctv.org/content/reportersblog/choices#:~:text=It's%20
estimated%20that%20the%20average,are%20both%20good%20and%20bad.

CHAPTER 5: WHY DO WE STRUGGLE?

BibleProject. "Overview: Job." October 22, 2015. Video, 11:00.
https://www.youtube.com/watch?v=xQwnH8th_fs&list=LLWuVCZ7TbNNpl_
rOcS7Qifg&index=1393.

Burns, Tyler. "Chadwick Boseman's faithful purpose showed from 'Black Panther' to
his dignified death." Religion News Service, August 31, 2020.
https://religionnews.com/2020/08/31/chadwick-bosemans-faithful-purpose-showed-
from-black-panther-to-his-dignified-death/.

Chan, Francis, and Lisa Chan. You and Me Forever: Marriage in Light of Eternity.
San Francisco: Claire Love Publishing, 2014. Kindle.

Goodreads,. "C.S. Lewis > Quotes > Quotable Quote." Accessed January 13, 2021.
https://www.goodreads.com/quotes/623193-we-can-ignore-even-pleasure-but-pain-
insists-upon-being.

CHAPTER 6: WAR, WRESTLING, & PASSION

Bible Hub. s.v. "3053. logismos." Bible Hub. Accessed January 27, 2021.
https://biblehub.com/greek/3053.htm.

The Gospel of Christ. "We Must Fight - Voddie Baucham | 01-16-2021." January 17, 2021. Video, 35:55.
https://www.youtube.com/watch?v=j8V3STNDA40&list=WL&index=2&ab_channel=TheGospelofChrist.

Luecke, Paul and Cecil Maranville. "Are Demons Real?." Life Hope & Truth. Accessed January 27, 2021.
https://lifehopeandtruth.com/prophecy/kingdom-of-god/god-vs-satan/are-demons-real/.

Nee, Watchman. The Spiritual Man. New York: Christian Fellowship Publishers, Inc, 1977.

Pinelli, Richard. "God vs. Satan: The Battle of the Ages." Life Hope & Truth. Accessed January 27, 2021.
https://lifehopeandtruth.com/prophecy/kingdom-of-god/god-vs-satan/.

CHAPTER 7: FULFILLMENT - WINNING
THE WAR ON PASSION

Baer, Drake. "How Mindfulness Went From Fringe To Mainstream." Thrive Global. Accessed February 2, 2021.
https://thriveglobal.com/stories/how-mindfulness-became-mainstream/#:~:text=It's%20all%20about%20evidence%2C%20says,of%20Mindfulness%2DBased%20Stress%20Reduction.&text=Image%20courtesy%20of%20Unsplash.,number%20jumped%20up%20to%2047.

Goodreads. "Ralph Waldo Emerson > Quotes > Quotable Quote." Accessed January 13, 2021.
https://www.goodreads.com/quotes/24142-life-is-a-journey-not-a-destination.

Ninivaggi, Frank John. "Why Has Mindfulness Become So Popular?" Psychology Today. Accessed February 2, 2021.
https://www.psychologytoday.com/us/blog/envy/201811/why-has-mindfulness-become-so-popular.

Quang Vu. "Question 9 Fulfillment." November 11, 2018. Video, 17:02.
https://www.youtube.com/watch?v=LEjKgRBaYIM&ab_channel=QuangVu.

CHAPTER 8: JOBS, CAREERS, CALLINGS, & PURPOSE

Groeschel, Craig. Chazown: Discover and Pursue God's Purpose for Your Life - Revised and Updated Edition. United States: Multnomah - The Crown Publishing Group, 2017.

Maxwell, John, and Mark Cole. "Calling and Purpose." September 1, 2020. In The John Maxwell Leadership Podcast. Produced by John C. Maxwell. Podcast, MP3 audio, 23:14.
https://open.spotify.com/episode/69rzDntXV7zGfiMgvPRhCR

Scazzero, Peter. Emotionally Healthy Spirituality: It's Impossible to be Spiritually Mature While Remaining Emotionally Immature, Updated Edition. Grand Rapids: Zondervan, 2017.

Wilding, Melody. "Do You Have a Job, Career or Calling? The Difference Matters."
Forbes, April 23, 2018.
https://www.forbes.com/sites/melodywilding/2018/04/23/do-you-have-a-job-career-
or-calling-the-difference-matters/?sh=7f553834632a.

CHAPTER 9: PURPOSE VS. DESTINY

Online Etymology Dictionary. s.v. "destiny (n.)." Online Etymology Dictionary.
Accessed February 2, 2021.
https://www.etymonline.com/word/destiny.

Online Etymology Dictionary. s.v. "purpose (n.)." Online Etymology Dictionary.
Accessed February 2, 2021.
https://www.etymonline.com/word/purpose.

Prager University. "Dennis Prager: Man's Search for Meaning by Viktor Frankl."
Accessed February 2, 2021.
https://www.prageru.com/video/dennis-prager-mans-search-for-meaning-by-
viktor-frankl/.

CHAPTER 11: KNOWING YOUR IDENTITY

Jon Leonetti. "Building our Lives on God." April 18, 2014. Video, 5:06.
https://www.youtube.com/watch?v=jANlYeK8a-A&ab_channel=JonLeonetti.

Leaf, Caroline. The Perfect You: A Blueprint for Identity. Grand Rapids: Baker
Publishing Group, 2017.

Scazzero, Peter. Emotionally Healthy Spirituality: It's Impossible to be Spiritually
Mature While Remaining Emotionally Immature, Updated Edition. Grand Rapids:
Zondervan, 2017.

CHAPTER 12: PASSION, PURPOSE, & THE INFECTED SOUL

Herbst, Dominic P. Restoring Relationships Resource Manual: "A Ministry of
Reconciliation." Ashburn: Sonrise House Company, 2005.

Restoring Relationships. "Marriage in Crisis." July 3, 2018. Video, 2:35.
https://www.youtube.com/watch?v=KYaXGRog2kQ&ab_
channel=RestoringRelationships.

CHAPTER 13: FORGIVENESS, RECONCILIATION, & PASSION

Bevere, John. The Bait of Satan. Lake Mary: Charisma House, 2014.

Bible Hub. s.v. "25. agapaó." Bible Hub. Accessed February 12, 2021.
https://biblehub.com/greek/25.htm.

Bible Hub. s.v. "2588. kardia." Bible Hub. Accessed February 12, 2021.
https://biblehub.com/greek/2588.htm.

Herbst, Dominic P. Restoring Relationships Resource Manual: "A Ministry of Reconciliation." Ashburn: Sonrise House Company, 2005.

Meyer, Joyce. Joyce Meyer Ministries (blog). "The Poison of Unforgiveness." Accessed February 12, 2021. https://joycemeyer.org/everydayanswers/ea-teachings/the-poison-of-unforgiveness.

CHAPTER 15: THE ART OF PASSIONEERING
Tebow, Tim. Tim Tebow (blog). "If You're Someone Who Always Listens to their Emotions, You Need to Stop." Accessed February 13, 2021. https://timtebow.com/blog/leading-conviction.

CHAPTER 16: OWNING YOUR STRUGGLES
Macron, Davis. The Right Messages. "31 Inspirational Quotes About Life and Struggles." October 1, 2018. Accessed February 15, 2021. https://therightmessages.com/life-and-struggles-quotes/.

Wiersbe, Warren W. Be Skillful: God's Guidebook to Wise Living. Colorado Springs: David C Cook, 2009.

CHAPTER 17: THE HOLY SPIRIT & YOU
Bevere, John. The Holy Spirit: An Introduction. Palmer Lake: Messenger International, 2013.

Google. "Empower." Accessed February 19, 2021. https://www.google.com/search?sxsrf=ALeKk03oewhhcdSQ69aRlknNgYbCMgS23Q%3A1613792938777&ei=qoYwYOLxLsOq1QHZjarIDQ&q=empower+definition&oq=empower+definition&gs_lcp=Cgdnd3Mtd2l6EAMyCQgjECcQRhD5ATICCAyAggAMgIIADICCAyBggAEBYQHjIGCAAQFhAeMgYIABAWEB4yBggAEBYQHjIGCAAQFhAeOgcIIxCwAxAnOgcIABCwAxBDOgUIABCxAzoHCAAQsQMQQzoICAAQsQMQgwE6BwgAEIcCEBQQsEMcBEK8BOgUIABCGCGA1DqDFiEFmDJFmgBcAJ4AIABwgSIAYUYkgELMi41LjEuMC4yLjGYAQCgAQGqAQdnd3Mtd2l6yAEKwAEB&sclient=gws-wiz&ved=oahUKEwji7uyWx_fuAhVDVDVTUKHdmGCtkQ4dUDCAo&uact=5.

The Religion Teacher. "The Meaning of Paraclete (Holy Spirit) in the Bible." June 11, 2019. Video, 2:14. https://www.youtube.com/watch?v=zg26V4i2ztQ&feature=youtu.be&ab_channel=TheReligionTeacher.

CHAPTER 18: THE PASSIONEER'S BLUEPRINTS
Bible Hub. s.v. "3618. oikodomeó." Accessed February 22, 2021. https://biblehub.com/greek/3618.htm.

Merriam-Webster. s.v. "Breathing Life Into 'Inspire': The word's origins are quite literal" Accessed January 13, 2021. https://www.merriam-webster.com/words-at-play/the-origins-of-inspire.

CHAPTER 19: THE FIRE WITHIN

BBC. "Saint Stephen." Accessed February 22, 2021. http://www.bbc.co.uk/religion/religions/christianity/saints/stephen. shtml#:~:text=When%20the%20number%20of%20disciples,who%20would%20 perform%20this%20task.

BibleProject. "Holy Spirit." April 5, 2017. Video, 4:10. https://www.youtube.com/watch?v=oNNZO9i1Gjc&feature=youtu.be&ab_ channel=BibleProject.

Bible Hub. s.v. "4442. pur." Accessed February 22, 2021. https://biblehub.com/greek/4442.htm.

Bible Hub. s.v. "4151. pneuma." Accessed February 22, 2021. https://biblehub.com/greek/4151.htm.

Bible Hub. s.v. "7307. ruach." Accessed February 22, 2021. https://biblehub.com/hebrew/7307.htm.

Maxwell, John C. The Maxwell Leadership Bible, NIV. Nashville: Thomas Nelson, 2018.

Merriam-Webster. s.v. "Sanhedrin." Accessed February 22, https://www.merriam-webster.com/dictionary/Sanhedrin.

CHAPTER 20: LOVE VS. FEAR

Bible Hub. s.v. "1167. deilia." Accessed February 22, 2021. https://biblehub.com/greek/1167.htm.

Bible Hub. s.v. "1169. deilos." Accessed February 22, 2021. https://biblehub.com/greek/1169.htm.

Bible Hub. s.v. "1411. dunamis." Accessed February 22, 2021. https://biblehub.com/greek/1411.htm.

Bible Hub. s.v. "1410. dunamai." Accessed February 22, 2021. https://biblehub.com/greek/1410.htm.

Bible Hub. s.v. "4995. sóphronismos." Accessed February 22, 2021. https://biblehub.com/greek/4995.htm.

Bible Hub. s.v. "4998. sóphrón." Accessed February 22, 2021. https://biblehub.com/greek/4998.htm.

Goodreads. "Maya Angelou > Quotes > Quotable Quote." Accessed January 13, 2021. https://www.goodreads.com/quotes/5934-i-ve-learned-that-people-will-forget-what-you-said-people#:~:text=%E2%80%9CI've%20learned%20that%20people%20 will%20forget%20what%20you%20said,how%20you%20made%20them%20 feel.%E2%80%9D.

CHAPTER 21: IMPACT - BEING A PASSIONEER

Maxwell, John, and Mark Cole. "Transformational Leadership (Part 1)." February 3, 2021. In The John Maxwell Leadership Podcast. Produced by John C. Maxwell. Podcast, MP3 audio, 34:58.
https://open.spotify.com/episode/7EK3W4490UrDgJehyDmeK4.

FINAL CHARGE

Goodreads, "Les Brown > Quotes > Quotable Quote." Accessed January 13, 2021. https://www.goodreads.com/quotes/623193-we-can-ignore-even-pleasure-but-pain-insists-upon-being.

RECOMMENDED RESOURCES

BOOKS

- *The Spiritual Man* by Watchman Nee

- *Experiencing God: Knowing and Doing the Will of God* by Henry and Richard Blackaby

- *The Holy Spirit: An Introduction* by John Bevere

- *The Maxwell Leadership Bible: Lessons in Leadership from the Word of God* by John C. Maxwell

- *Switch on Your Brain: The Key to Peak Happiness, Thinking, and Health* by Dr. Caroline Leaf

- *How Successful People Think* by John C. Maxwell.

- *The Passion and the Cross* by Ronald Rolheiser

- *Christian Disciplines: Building Strong Christian Character through Divine Guidance, Suffering, Peril, Prayer, Loneliness, and Patience* by Oswald Chambers

- *Soul Care: 7 Transformational Principles for a Healthy Soul* by Dr. Rob Reimer

- *Crazy Love: Overwhelmed by a Relentless God* by Francis Chan

- *The Leader's Palette: Seven Primary Colors* by Ralph E. Enlow Jr.

COUNSELING & DISCIPLESHIP PROGRAMS
- Restoring Relationships by Dominic Herbst

    a. visit restoringrelationships.org for more information

- Emotionally Healthy Spirituality & Relationships by Pete & Geri Scazzero

    a. visit emotionallyhealthy.org for more information

ACKNOWLEDGMENTS

The best way to describe the process of writing this book is that of a long wrestling match. There were times I was on top of it and fully enjoying the journey, and then there were countless days and weeks where everything within me wanted to throw in the towel and simply focus on all of the other priorities in my life.

I have so many people to thank for the Passioneering they have provided to me throughout this incredible and challenging journey. From prayers and words of encouragement to checking in on me during early mornings and late evenings, I realized pretty quickly one of the most important parts of writing a book is to not do it alone, but invite others on your journey so they can inspire, encourage, and empower you when your own motivation begins to weaken.

Thank you to those who have been in my life for a season, a reason, or a lifetime who have guided, molded, and shaped me into who I am today. This book is truly a culmination of many life experiences and encounters with beautiful souls.

God—thank you for burdening me with this vision and for never letting me give up. It is my hope that this book honors you and brings countless others closer into relationship with you. Wherever you lead, I will go.

Mom—thank you for encouraging me to always dream big and aim high and for your unconditional love.

Dad—thank you for being one of the first Passioneers in my life and thank you for your unwavering support of all God has called me to do.

Jonathan—my brother! Your faith in me and support in making this book a reality is something I will always be grateful for. Thank you for always having my back throughout life.

Mana & DeeDee—thank you for instilling within me the values of respect, consideration, and integrity, and thank you for modeling what it means to truly work hard and always put others before yourself.

Toby—my pup! You've seen the good, the bad, and the ugly throughout this journey. Thank you for always being in the same room with me as I wrote so I was never alone in this process, and thank you for nudging me for playtime when I needed a break. I cherish your companionship.

Thank you to the team at New Degree Press for their consistent aid, confidence, and empowerment in helping me bring this book to fruition. Thank you to Eric Koester and Brian Bies for developing an awesome program that inspires, encourages, and empowers individuals to become first-time authors, and a special shout out goes to my editors Jesse Rivas and Cynthia Tucker. Your steadfast encouragement and confidence in my vision truly empowered me throughout the way.

Finally, thank you to the many below who have intentionally invested in me by pre-ordering a book and making this book truly become a reality. May you share in the legacy of the impact that God wills to have through this book.

Abby Cowser

Abby Krehl

Abraham Benguigui

Adam Troy Bannister

Alec Broniszewski

Alex Greenawalt

Alex Lopresti

Alexandra Masters

Allison Hedin

Amanda McIlvain

Amy Acierno

Andrew Reidlinger

Angelina Russo

Anne Magliola

Annie Hepner

Bridget Black

Bryan Burkentine

Chris DeSantis

Christine Grezeszak

Christopher Bonczak

Christopher DeSantis

Claire Gauthier

Cullen Raftery

Cynthia Tucker

Daniel Calderon

Daniel Hadas

Daniel Shashaty

Daniel Stauffer

Daniel Zirtzman

Dareen Romanchik

David Charles Mewkalo II

David & Naomi Mezzacappa

Debbie D'Addio

DJ & Nicole Bennett

Donna Antice

Donna Dawson

Doug Uhazie

Drew Kerr

Elizabeth Mummert

Emily Roarty

Eric Koester

Eric McCall

Felix Dey

Frances Vicario

Frank Henry

Fran McDermid

George Henning

Gina Farkouh

Giuseppe Scire

Glenn Bird

Gloria Mezzacappa

Grace McClellan

Graham Smith

Haley McClain Hill

Hannah Greider

Hannah Maddox

Isabella Webster

Jack Boylan

Jackie Mezzacappa

Jackie Nunes

Jacob Rausch

James Pipitone

Jennifer Ahern

Jesse Rivas

Jessica McCarter

Jessica Smith

Joanne Bianchi

Jodi Rennie

Joe Battista

Joe & Maria Marzella

John Davis

John Feret

John Mezzacappa

John Shagan

John Wiater

Jonathan Mezzacappa

Joseph Persichetti

Kara Wiberg

Katherine DeFiore

Katie Oomkes

Kelly Hanley

Kenny & Lynda Mezzacappa

Kylene Cochrane

Labeed Almani

Lauren Donatelli

Lauren J Boyle

Lesli Rice

Louis Valerio

Lydia Herring

Madeline R Bailey

Maria Longobardi

Marie Ribaudo

Mark Jackson

Mark Keck

Marianne Mezzacappa

Matthew Hoffman

Matthew Terrone

Mike & Peggy Buttermark

Michael Savchuck

Michelle Bruni

Misha Demchuk

Nathaniel Weger

Nicholas Darr

Nichole Powers

Nick Brady

Nikki Mayers

Nolan Amos

Patrick Prior

Paul & Yolanda Vicario

Phyliss Esposito

Rachel Reiss

Rebecca McGowan

Robert Miller

Rocco Del Priore

Rosalie Bueti

Ryan Rudalavage

Ryan Steinberg

Salem Alakbari

Sarah Amendolare

Sarah Custer

Sarah Snyder

Sarena Mezzacappa

Savannah Washlesky

Sean Dobson

Shelby Nease

Simone Yaghi

Steve & Moe Skidmore

Steven Longobardi

Steven Waldman

Taylor Henry

Taylor Sweeney

Terri Hartman

Thomas Mezzacappa

Thomas Nylec

Thomas Shashaty

Timothy & Elizabeth Daigle

Tom & Mary Drabik

Tristen Black

Vanessa Robinson

Victor DeMaio

Vincent Fiorenza